Zabbix Cookbook

Over 70 hands-on recipes to get your infrastructure up and running with Zabbix

Patrik Uytterhoeven

PUBLISHING

BIRMINGHAM - MUMBAI

Zabbix Cookbook

First published: March 2015

Production reference: 1110315

Published by Packt Publishing Ltd.
Livery Place
35 Livery Street
Birmingham B3 2PB, UK.

ISBN 978-1-78439-758-6

www.packtpub.com

Credits

Author

Patrik Uytterhoeven

Reviewers

Sankar Bheemarasetty

Siju Oommen George

Luke MacNeil

Commissioning Editor

Amarabha Banerjee

Acquisition Editor

Nikhil Karkal

Content Development Editor

Sweny M. Sukumaran

Technical Editor

Tanmayee Patil

Copy Editors

Vikrant Phadke

Aarti Saldanha

Project Coordinator

Akash Poojary

Proofreaders

Simran Bhogal

Clyde Jenkins

Chris Smith

Indexer

Priya Sane

Graphics

Abhinash Sahu

Production Coordinator

Shantanu N. Zagade

Cover Work

Shantanu N. Zagade

About the Author

Patrik Uytterhoeven has over 16 years of experience in IT. Most of this time was spent on HP Unix and Red Hat Linux. In late 2012, he joined Open-Future, a leading open source integrator and the first Zabbix reseller and training partner in Belgium.

When Patrik joined Open-Future, he gained the opportunity to certify himself as a Zabbix Certified Trainer. Since then, he has provided trainings and public demonstrations not only in Belgium but also around the world, in countries such as the Netherlands, Germany, Canada, and Ireland.

Because Patrik also has a deep interest in configuration management, he wrote some Ansible roles for Red Hat 6.x and 7.x to deploy and update Zabbix. These roles, and some others, can be found in the Ansible Galaxy at `https://galaxy.ansible.com/list#/users/1375`.

Patrik is also a technical reviewer of *Learning Ansible* and the upcoming book, *Ansible Configuration Management*, both published by Packt Publishing.

I would like to thank my colleague Tom for helping me reviewing the book. I would also like to thank my girlfriend Mui who had to spend countless evenings alone before TV when I was writing this book. I would also like to thank Open-Future the company I work for as they gave me the time that was needed to for this book and at last I would like to thank all the reviewers for the ideas and feedback and the people from PacktLib. Without them this book would never have been possible.

About the Reviewers

Sankar Bheemarasetty is doing his master's at Technische Universität Darmstadt, Germany. He worked as a systems engineer for more than 3 and a half years on various technologies and programming languages. Zabbix is one of the monitoring solutions he has worked on. Bheemarasetty completed his bachelor's degree in information technology at VIT University, Vellore, India. Experimenting with new technologies is his hobby. You can contact him at www.learnsomuch.com and http://learnsomuch.github.io/.

I would like to thank my dad, mom, brother, and sister, who have always supported me. I'd also like to thank the author—Patrik Uytterhoeven—Packt Publishing, and its staff for giving me the opportunity to contribute to this project.

Siju Oommen George works as the chief information security officer with ZestyBeanz Technologies. He oversees the data visualization, cloud computing, security auditing, and digital forensics departments, and is active in research. He is also involved in several product development initiatives of the company.

Siju completed his BTech course in production engineering from the University of Calicut in 2000 and worked in the systems administration department of HIFX (hifx.co.in) for 15 years. During this period, he learned technologies such as BSDs, OS X, Linux, cloud computing, and Microsoft Windows platforms involving both open source and proprietary software. He has written articles (https://www.linkedin.com/today/author/57177969) for BSD Magazine and has contributed to many open source mailing lists. He is an advocate of open source software and encourages newcomers by mentoring them.

Siju also reviews books in his spare time. Earlier, he reviewed *Squid Proxy Server 3.1 Beginner's Guide*, *Packt Publishing*.

I would like to thank my Lord and savior, Jesus Christ, who carried me thus far and gave success in my career, regardless of the sickness I continually struggle with. I would also like to thank my wife, Sophia, and daughter, Manahane, for bearing the burdens I put on them.

Luke MacNeil is a 32-year-old Linux engineer and developer from Massachusetts. He has worked on scalable Linux and *nix systems and the development of web-based system administration tools for the last 10 years. He spends his free time on `irc.freenode.net` (`#linuxpeople`) along with a handful of other open source professionals, sharing mostly "yo mama" jokes and internet memes in the middle of the night. Currently, Luke is expanding his knowledge of complex cloud computing at `https://www.salesforce.com/`. Some of his other interests include audio production, guitar repairs, songwriting, and hosting an open mic at the Rose Garden restaurant in Upton, Massachusetts, where he can be found every Thursday night (provided he is not out in a hotel room playing with golang in San Francisco).

I'd like to thank my mother, Lynn Leblanc-MacNeil, as well as my girlfriend, Jennifer Crawford, for their support throughout the many years of my antisocial geek-like behavior.

www.PacktPub.com

Support files, eBooks, discount offers, and more

For support files and downloads related to your book, please visit www.PacktPub.com.

Did you know that Packt offers eBook versions of every book published, with PDF and ePub files available? You can upgrade to the eBook version at www.PacktPub.com and as a print book customer, you are entitled to a discount on the eBook copy. Get in touch with us at service@packtpub.com for more details.

At www.PacktPub.com, you can also read a collection of free technical articles, sign up for a range of free newsletters and receive exclusive discounts and offers on Packt books and eBooks.

https://www2.packtpub.com/books/subscription/packtlib

Do you need instant solutions to your IT questions? PacktLib is Packt's online digital book library. Here, you can search, access, and read Packt's entire library of books.

Why Subscribe?

- ► Fully searchable across every book published by Packt
- ► Copy and paste, print, and bookmark content
- ► On demand and accessible via a web browser

Free Access for Packt account holders

If you have an account with Packt at www.PacktPub.com, you can use this to access PacktLib today and view 9 entirely free books. Simply use your login credentials for immediate access.

Table of Contents

Preface

Since its first release in 2001, Zabbix has distinguished itself from other monitoring solutions by providing great flexibility and performance. Hence, it is being used more and more by large companies. This doesn't mean Zabbix can't be used in smaller setups. As mentioned before, Zabbix is a very flexible monitoring tool that can start small and grow big. Monitoring more than 100,000 devices with Zabbix is no issue at all.

This book will show you how to set up Zabbix and configure it to your needs, be it in a small or a large setup.

What this book covers

Chapter 1, Zabbix Configuration, covers the entire installation of Zabbix from scratch. This includes installation of the Zabbix server and agent. At the end of this chapter is the procedure to install Zabbix in a distributed way.

Chapter 2, Getting Around in Zabbix, helps you discover the frontend, explains the Zabbix definitions, and shows you how to acknowledge triggers. To give you a better understanding of what is possible with your Zabbix setup, this chapter goes a bit deeper into the Zabbix architecture.

Chapter 3, Groups, Users, and Permissions, explains how to create hosts in Zabbix and split them in groups. This chapter also covers how to create users and user groups. Then it explains the different ways to authenticate and administer Zabbix.

Chapter 4, Monitoring with Zabbix, takes you to the next logical step— explaining every item that can be created in Zabbix, by making use of easy-to-follow recipes.

Chapter 5, Testing with Triggers in Zabbix, shows you how to build triggers in an easy way with the trigger constructor. This chapter also covers how to build more advanced triggers and how to test them.

Chapter 6, *Working with Templates*, explains what templates are and how to create, link, and nest them in Zabbix. This chapter also teaches you how to make use of macros in your templates.

Chapter 7, *Data Visualization and Reporting in Zabbix*, explains the different ways to visualize data in Zabbix by making use of graphs, screens, slideshows, and maps. This chapter also covers how to create reports and SLA reports in Zabbix.

Chapter 8, *Monitoring VMware and Proxies*, shows you how to monitor your VMware infrastructure. Then this chapter explains the different kinds of proxies and how to use them for monitoring.

Chapter 9, *Autodiscovery*, demonstrates how to discover hosts on your network with Zabbix and perform automation after the discovery. This chapter also introduces automatic registration of active agents and low-level discovery of items.

Chapter 10, *Zabbix Maintenance and API*, explains how to place hosts in your Zabbix in maintenance mode. This chapter also covers internal items in Zabbix, what to back up, and some performance considerations. Last but not least, it covers the Zabbix API and shows you how to add hosts with the API using examples.

Appendix, *Upgrading and Troubleshooting Zabbix*, is an overview demonstrating how to upgrade your installation, how to troubleshoot Zabbix, and some best practices to follow. This chapter teaches you some guidelines and talks about the upcoming Zabbix version. It also shows you how to interact with the community, as this will probably be the first point of contact when there are Zabbix-related issues.

What you need for this book

It is important to know that in this book, we've made use of Red Hat Enterprise 6.x or one of the forks such as CentOS. Most recipes will work on other distributions as well but, in some cases, you'll probably have to look for files in other locations. Where possible the book has been updated for the latest Red Hat release v7 as Zabbix support was added during the progress of this book.

In this book, we will show you how to monitor an IPMI device with Zabbix. Obviously, you'll need an IPMI-capable device, and the same goes for SNMP monitoring. In *Chapter 8*, *Monitoring VMware and Proxies*, we will talk about VMware monitoring. For that, you need to have VMware vCenter 4.1 or a later version.

Who this book is for

This book focuses on system administrators who have some basic experience or no experience at all with Zabbix. This book will guide you from the setup until getting messages about problems that have been found by Zabbix. It will be useful if you have some programming skills because in *Chapter 10, Zabbix Maintenance and API*, we'll talk about the API; but for the rest of the book, no programming skills are needed. This book shows you how to create items to monitor IPMI- and SNMP-capable devices, databases, and so on. Hence, wide knowledge of IT is certainly useful if you would like to learn how to monitor with Zabbix. After all, you need to understand first what you want to monitor before learning how to monitor it.

Conventions

In this book, you will find a number of styles of text that distinguish between different kinds of information. Here are some examples of these styles, and explanations of their meanings.

Code words in text, database table names, folder names, filenames, file extensions, pathnames, dummy URLs, user input, and Twitter handles are shown as follows: "Save the file in the /usr/src folder."

A block of code is set as follows:

```
# vi /etc/zabbix/zabbix_server.conf
DBHost=localhost
DBName=zabbix
```

Any command-line input or output is written as follows:

```
# yum install mysql-server zabbix-server-mysql
```

New terms and **important words** are shown in bold. Words that you see on the screen, in menus or dialog boxes for example, appear in the text like this: "The **Media** tab is the place where the user can add the media that he or she wants to use to get notifications."

 Warnings or important notes appear in a box like this.

Tips and tricks appear like this.

Reader feedback

Feedback from our readers is always welcome. Let us know what you think about this book—what you liked or may have disliked. Reader feedback is important for us to develop titles that you really get the most out of.

To send us general feedback, simply send an e-mail to feedback@packtpub.com, and mention the book title via the subject of your message.

If there is a topic that you have expertise in and you are interested in either writing or contributing to a book, see our author guide on www.packtpub.com/authors.

Customer support

Now that you are the proud owner of a Packt book, we have a number of things to help you to get the most from your purchase.

Errata

Although we have taken every care to ensure the accuracy of our content, mistakes do happen. If you find a mistake in one of our books—maybe a mistake in the text or the code—we would be grateful if you would report this to us. By doing so, you can save other readers from frustration and help us improve subsequent versions of this book. If you find any errata, please report them by visiting http://www.packtpub.com/submit-errata, selecting your book, clicking on the **Errata Submission Form** link, and entering the details of your errata. Once your errata are verified, your submission will be accepted and the errata will be uploaded on our website, or added to any list of existing errata, under the Errata section of that title.

To view the previously submitted errata, go to https://www.packtpub.com/books/content/support and enter the name of the book in the search field. The required information will appear under the **Errata** section.

Piracy

Piracy of copyright material on the Internet is an ongoing problem across all media. At Packt, we take the protection of our copyright and licenses very seriously. If you come across any illegal copies of our works, in any form, on the Internet, please provide us with the location address or website name immediately so that we can pursue a remedy.

Please contact us at copyright@packtpub.com with a link to the suspected pirated material.

We appreciate your help in protecting our authors, and our ability to bring you valuable content.

Questions

You can contact us at questions@packtpub.com if you are having a problem with any aspect of the book, and we will do our best to address it.

1
Zabbix Configuration

In this chapter we will cover the following topics:

- ► Server installation and configuration
- ► Agent installation and configuration
- ► Frontend installation and configuration
- ► Installing Zabbix from source
- ► Installing the server in a distributed setup

Introduction

We will begin with the installation and configuration of a Zabbix server, Zabbix agent, and web interface. We will make use of our package manager for the installation. Not only will we show you how to install and configure Zabbix, we will also show you how to compile everything from source. We will also cover the installation of the Zabbix server in a distributed way.

Server installation and configuration

Here we will explain how to install and configure the Zabbix server, along with the prerequisites.

Getting ready

To get started with this chapter, we need a properly configured server, with a Red Hat 6.x or 7.x 64-bit OS installed or a derivate such as CentOS. The book was written with version 6 but the commands have been updated for version 7, where needed.

It is possible to get the installation working on other distributions such as SUSE, Debian, Ubuntu, or another Linux distribution, but in this book I will be focusing on Red Hat based systems. I feel that it's the best choice for this book as the OS is not only available for big companies willing to pay Red Hat for support, but also for those smaller companies that cannot afford to pay for it, or for those just willing to test it or run it with community support. Other distros like Debian, Ubuntu, SUSE, OpenBSD will work fine too but the book would end up all cluttered with different kinds of setups for each distro. It is possible to run Zabbix on 32-bit systems, but I will only focus on 64-bit installations as 64-bit is probably what you will run in a production setup. However if you want to try it on 32-bit system, it is perfectly possible with the use of the Zabbix 32-bit binaries.

How to do it...

The following steps will guide you through the server installation process:

1. The first thing we need to do is add the Zabbix repository to our package manager on our server so that we are able to download the Zabbix packages to set up our server. To find the latest repository, go to the Zabbix webpage www.zabbix.com and click on **Product | Documentation** then select the latest version. At the time of this writing, it is version 2.4.

2. From the manual, select option **3 Installation**, then go to option **3 Installation from packages** and follow instructions to install the Zabbix repository. For Zabbix 2.4.x, it will appear like this:

```
[root@zabbix ~]# rpm -ivh http://repo.zabbix.com/zabbix/2.4/rhel/6/x86_64/zabbix-release-2.4-1.el6.noarch.rpm
Retrieving http://repo.zabbix.com/zabbix/2.4/rhel/6/x86_64/zabbix-release-2.4-1.el6.noarch.rpm
Preparing...                ########################################### [100%]
   1:zabbix-release          ########################################### [100%]
[root@zabbix ~]#
```

Now that our Zabbix repository is installed, we can continue with our installation. For our Zabbix server to work, we will also need a database for example: MySQL, PostgreSQL, Oracle and a web server for the frontend such as Apache, Nginx, and so on. In our setup, we will install Apache and MySQL as they are better known and easiest to set up. We will later see some alternatives in our book and how to install our server in a distributed way, but for now let's just keep things simple.

There is a bit of a controversy around MySQL that was acquired by Oracle some time ago. Since then, most of the original developers left and forked the project. Those forks have also made major improvements over MySQL. It could be a good alternative to make use of MariaDB or Percona. In **Red Hat Enterprise Linux** (**RHEL**) 7.x, MySQL has been replace already by MariaDB.

```
http://www.percona.com/.
https://mariadb.com/.
http://www.zdnet.com/article/stallman-admits-gpl-
flawed-proprietary-licensing-needed-to-pay-for-mysql-
development/.
```

The following steps will show you how to install the MySQL server and the Zabbix server with a MySQL connection:

```
# yum install mysql-server zabbix-server-mysql
# yum install mariadb-server zabbix-server-mysql (for RHEL 7)
# service mysqld start
# systemctl start mariadb.service (for RHEL 7)
# /usr/bin/mysql_secure_installation
```

In this book, we make use of MySQL because it is what most people know best and use most of the time. It is also easier to set up than PostgreSQL for most people. However, a MySQL DB will not shrink in size. It's probably wise to use PostgreSQL instead, as PostgreSQL has a housekeeper process that cleans up the database. However, in very large setups this housekeeper process of PostgreSQL can at times also be the problem of slowness. When this happens, a deeper understanding of how housekeeper works is needed.

MySQL will come and ask us some questions here so make sure you read the next lines before you continue:

1. For the MySQL secure installation, we are being asked to give the current root password or press **Enter** if you don't have one. This is the root password for MySQL and we don't have one yet as we did a clean installation of MySQL. So you can just press **Enter** here.

2. Next question will be to set a root password; best thing is of course, to set a MySQL root password. Make it a complex one and store it safe in a program such as KeePass or Password Safe.

3. After the root password is set, MySQL will prompt you to remove anonymous users. You can select **Yes** and let MySQL remove them.

4. We also don't need any remote login of root users, so best is to disallow remote login for the root user as well.

5. For our production environment, we don't need any test databases left on our server. So those can also be removed from our machine and finally we do a reload of the privileges.

You can now continue with the rest of the configuration by configuring our database and starting all the services. This way we make sure they will come up again when we restart our server:

```
# mysql -u root -p
```

```
mysql> create database zabbix character set utf8 collate utf8_bin;
mysql> grant all privileges on zabbix.* to zabbix@localhost identified by
'<some-safe-password>';
mysql> exit;
```

```
# cd /usr/share/doc/zabbix-server-mysql-2.4.x/create
# mysql -u zabbix -p zabbix < schema.sql
# mysql -u zabbix -p zabbix < images.sql
# mysql -u zabbix -p zabbix < data.sql
```

 Depending on the speed of your machine, importing the schema could take some time (a few minutes). It's important to not mix the order of the import of the SQL files!

1. Now let's edit the Zabbix server configuration file and add our database settings in it:
   ```
   # vi /etc/zabbix/zabbix_server.conf
   DBHost=localhost
   DBName=zabbix
   DBUser=zabbix
   DBPassword=<some-safe-password>
   ```

2. Let's start our Zabbix server and make sure it will come online together with the MySQL database after reboot:
   ```
   # service zabbix-server start
   # chkconfig zabbix-server on
   # chkconfig mysqld on
   ```

On RHEL 7 this will be:

```
# systemctl start zabbix-server
# systemctl enable zabbix-server
# systemctl enable mariadb
```

3. Check now if our server was started correctly:

    ```
    # tail /var/log/zabbix/zabbix_server.log
    ```

    The output would look something like this:

    ```
    # 1788:20140620:231430.274 server #7 started [poller #5]
    # 1804:20140620:231430.276 server #19 started [discoverer #1]
    ```

    If no errors where displayed in the log, your `zabbix-server` is online. In case you have errors, they will probably look like this:

    ```
        1589:20150106:211530.180 [Z3001] connection to database 'zabbix'
    failed: [1045] Access denied for user 'zabbix'@'localhost' (using
    password: YES)
        1589:20150106:211530.180 database is down: reconnecting in 10
    seconds
    ```

    In this case, go back to the `zabbix_server.conf` file and check the `DBHost`, `DBName`, `DBUser`, and `DBPassword` parameters again to see if they are correct.

    The only thing that needs to be done is editing the firewalld. Add the following line in the `/etc/sysconfig/iptables` file under the line with `dport 22`. This can be done with vi or Emacs or another editor such as: the `vi /etc/sysconfig/iptables` file. If you would like to know more about iptables have a look at the CentOS wiki (link provided in *See also* section).

    ```
    # -A INPUT -m state --state NEW -m tcp -p tcp --dport 10051 -j
    ACCEPT
    ```

    People making use of RHEL 7 have firewall and need to run following commands instead.

    ```
    # firewall-cmd --permanent --add-port=10051/tcp
    ```

4. Now that this is done, you can reload the firewall. The Zabbix server is installed and we are ready to continue to the installation of the agent and the frontend.

    ```
    # service iptables restart
    # firewall-cmd --reload (For users of RHEL 7)
    ```

    Always check if the ports `10051` and `10050` are also in your `/etc/services` file both server and agent are IANA registered.

How it works...

The installation we have done here is just for the Zabbix server and the database. We still need to add an agent and a frontend with a web server.

The Zabbix server will communicate through the local socket with the MySQL database. Later, we will see how we can change this if we want to install MySQL on another server than our Zabbix server.

The Zabbix server needs a database to store its configuration and the received data, for which we have installed a MySQL database. Remember we did a `create database` and named it `zabbix`? Then we did a grant on the `zabbix` database and we gave all privileges on this database to a user with the name `zabbix` with some free to choose password `<some-safe-password>`. After the creation of the database we had to upload three files namely `schema.sql`, `images.sql`, and `data.sql`. Those files contain the database structure and data for the Zabbix server to work. It is very important that you keep the correct order when you upload them to your database. The next thing we did was adjusting the `zabbix_server.conf` file; this is needed to let our Zabbix server know what database we have used with what credentials and where the location is.

The next thing we did was starting the Zabbix server and making sure that with a reboot, both MySQL and the Zabbix server would start up again.

Our final step was to check the log file to see if the Zabbix server was started without any errors and the opening of TCP `port 10051` in the firewall. `Port 10051` is the port being used by Zabbix active agents to communicate with the server. In Chapter 4, we will go deeper and understand the difference of active and passive agents. For now just remember, an agent can be either active or passive in Zabbix.

There's more...

We have changed some settings for the communication with our database in the `/etc/zabbix/zabbix_server.conf` file but there are many more options in this file to set. So let's have a look at which are the other options that we can change. Some of them will probably sound like a foreign language to you but don't worry, it will all become more clear later in this book.

The following URL gives us an overview of all supported parameters in the `zabbix_server.conf` file:

```
https://www.zabbix.com/documentation/2.4/manual/appendix/config/
zabbix_server.
```

You can start the server with another configuration file so you can experiment with multiple configuration settings. This can be useful if you like to experiment with certain options. To do this, run the following command where the `<config file>` file is another `zabbix_server.conf` file than the original file:

```
zabbix_server -c <config file>
```

See also

▸ http://www.greensql.com/content/mysql-security-best-practices-hardening-mysql-tips

▸ http://passwordsafe.sourceforge.net/

▸ http://keepass.info/

▸ http://www.fpx.de/fp/Software/Gorilla/

▸ http://wiki.centos.org/HowTos/Network/IPTables

Agent installation and configuration

In this section, we will explain you the installation and configuration of the Zabbix agent. The Zabbix agent is a small piece of software about 700 KB in size. You will need to install this agent on all your servers to be able to monitor the local resources with Zabbix.

Getting ready

In this recipe, to get our Zabbix agent installed, we need to have our server with the Zabbix server up and running as explained in *Server installation and configuration*. In this setup, we will install our agent first on the Zabbix server. We just make use of the Zabbix server in this setup to install a server that can monitor itself. If you monitor another server then there is no need to install a Zabbix server, only the agent is enough.

How to do it...

Installing the Zabbix agent is quite easy once our server has been set up. The first thing we need to do is install the agent package.

Installing the agent packages can be done by running `yum` as we have already added the repository to our package manager in the previous recipe *Server installation and configuration*. In case you have skipped it, then go back and add the Zabbix repository to your package manager.

1. Install the Zabbix agent from the package manager:

    ```
    # yum install zabbix-agent
    ```

2. Open the correct port in your firewall. The Zabbix server communicates to the agent if the agent is passive. So, if your agent is on a server other than Zabbix, then we need to open the firewall on port 10050. (We shall further explain active and passive agents in Chapter 4).

3. Edit the firewall, open the file `/etc/sysconfig/iptables` and add the following after the line with `dport 22` in the next line:

    ```
    # -A INPUT -m state --state NEW -m tcp -p tcp --dport 10050 -j
    ACCEPT
    ```

4. Users of RHEL 7 can run:

    ```
    # firewall-cmd --permanent --add-port=10050/tcp
    ```

5. Now that the firewall is adjusted, you can restart the same:

    ```
    # service iptables restart
    # firewall-cmd --reload (if you use RHEL 7)
    ```

    The only thing left to do is edit the `zabbix_agentd.conf` file, start the agent, and make sure it starts after a reboot.

6. Edit the Zabbix agent configuration file and add or change the following settings. We will see later in Chapter 4 the difference between active and passive; for now just fill in both variables.

    ```
    # vi /etc/zabbix/zabbix_agentd.conf

    Server=<ip of the zabbix server>

    ServerActive=<ip of the zabbix server>
    ```

    That's all for now in order to edit in the `zabbix_agentd.conf` file.

7. Now, let's start the Zabbix agent:

    ```
    # service zabbix-agent start
    # systemctl start zabbix-agent (if you use RHEL 7)
    ```

8. And finally make sure that our agent will come online after a reboot:

    ```
    # chkconfig zabbix-agent on
    # systemctl enable zabbix-agent (for RHEL 7 users)
    ```

9. Check again that there are no errors in the log file from the agent:

```
# tail /var/log/zabbix/zabbix_agentd.log
```

How it works...

The agent we have installed is installed from the Zabbix repository on the Zabbix server, and communicates to the server on `port 10051` if we make use of an active agent. If we make use of a passive agent, then our Zabbix server will talk to the Zabbix agent on `port 10050`. Remember that our agent is installed locally on our host; so all communication stays on our server. This is not the case if our agent is installed on another server instead of our Zabbix server. We have edited the configuration file from the agent and changed the `Server` and `ServerActive` options. Our Zabbix agent is now ready to communicate with our Zabbix server. Based on the two parameters we have changed, the agent knows what the IP is from the Zabbix server.

The difference between passive and active modes is that the client in passive mode will wait for the Zabbix server to ask for data from the Zabbix agent.

The agent in active mode will ask the server first what it needs to monitor and pull this data from the Zabbix server. From that moment on, the Zabbix agent will send the values by itself to the server at regular intervals.

So when we use a passive agent the Zabbix server pulls the data from the agent where a active agent pushes the data to the server.

We did not change the `hostname` item in the `zabbix_agentd.conf` file, a parameter we normally need to change and give the host a unique name. In our case the name in the agent will already be in the Zabbix server that we have installed, so there is no need to change it this time.

There's more...

Just like our server, the agent has a plenty more options to set in its configuration file. So open the file again and have a look at what else we can adjust. In the following URLs you will find all options that can be changed in the Zabbix agent configuration file for Unix and Windows:

https://www.zabbix.com/documentation/2.4/manual/appendix/config/zabbix_agentd.

https://www.zabbix.com/documentation/2.4/manual/appendix/config/zabbix_agentd_win.

Frontend installation and configuration

In this recipe, we will finalize our setup with the installation and configuration of the Zabbix web interface. Our Zabbix configuration is different from other monitoring tools such as Nagios in the way that the complete configuration is stored in a database. This means, that we need a web interface to be able to configure and work with the Zabbix server. It is not possible to work without the web interface and just make use of some text files to do the configuration. It is however possible to work with the API, but that is something we will see later in Chapter 10.

Getting ready

To be successful with this installation, you need to have installed the Zabbix server, as explained previously. It's not necessary to have the Zabbix client installed but it is recommended. This way, we can monitor our Zabbix server because we have a Zabbix agent running on our Zabbix server. This can be useful in monitoring your own Zabbix servers health status, as we will see later.

How to do it...

1. The first thing we need to do is go back to our prompt and install the Zabbix web frontend packages.

   ```
   # yum install zabbix-web zabbix-web-mysql
   ```

2. With the installation of our Zabbix-web package, Apache was installed too, so we need to start Apache first and make sure it will come online after a reboot:

   ```
   # chkconfig httpd on; service start httpd
   # systemctl start httpd; systemctl enable httpd (for RHEL 7)
   ```

3. Remember we have a firewall, so the same rule applies here. We need to open the port for the web server to be able to see our Zabbix frontend. Edit the /etc/sysconfig/iptables firewall file and add after the line with dport 22 in the next line:

   ```
   # -A INPUT -m state –state NEW -m tcp -p tcp –dport 80 -j ACCEPT
   ```

If iptables is too intimidating for you, then an alternative could to make use of **Shorewall**. http://www.cyberciti.biz/faq/centos-rhel-shorewall-firewall-configuration-setup-howto-tutorial/.

Users of RHEL 7 can run the following lines:

```
# firewall-cmd --permanent --add-service=http
```

The following screenshot shows the firewall configuration:

```
# Firewall configuration written by system-config-firewall
# Manual customization of this file is not recommended.
*filter
:INPUT ACCEPT [0:0]
:FORWARD ACCEPT [0:0]
:OUTPUT ACCEPT [0:0]
-A INPUT -m state --state ESTABLISHED,RELATED -j ACCEPT
-A INPUT -p icmp -j ACCEPT
-A INPUT -i lo -j ACCEPT
-A INPUT -m state --state NEW -m tcp -p tcp --dport 22 -j ACCEPT
-A INPUT -m state --state NEW -m tcp -p tcp --dport 80 -j ACCEPT
-A INPUT -j REJECT --reject-with icmp-host-prohibited
-A FORWARD -j REJECT --reject-with icmp-host-prohibited
COMMIT
```

4. Now that the firewall is adjusted, you can save and restart the firewall:

```
# iptables-save
# service iptables restart
# firewall-cmd --reload (If you run RHEL 7)
```

5. Now edit the Zabbix configuration file with the PHP setting. Uncomment the option for the timezone and fill in the correct timezone:

```
# vi /etc/httpd/conf.d/zabbix.conf
php_value date.timezone Europe/Brussels
```

6. It is now time to reboot our server and see if everything comes back online with our Zabbix server configured like we intended it to. The reboot here is not necessary but it's a good test to see if we did a correct configuration of our server:

```
# reboot
```

7. Now let's see if we get to see our Zabbix server. Go to the URL of our Zabbix server that we just have installed:

```
# http://<ip of the Zabbix server>/zabbix
```

8. On the first page, we see our welcome screen. Here, we can just click **Next**:

The standard Zabbix installation will run on port 80, although It isn't really a safe solution. It would be better to make use of HTTPS. However, this is a bit out of the scope of this book but could be done with not too much extra work and would make Zabbix more safe. `http://wiki.centos.org/HowTos/Https`.

ZABBIX

1. Welcome

2. Check of pre-requisites

3. Configure DB connection

4. Zabbix server details

5. Pre-Installation summary

6. Install

Welcome to
Zabbix 2.4

www.zabbix.com
Licensed under GPL v2

Cancel

Next »

9. Next screen, Zabbix will do a check of the PHP settings. Normally they should be fine as Zabbix provides a file with all correct settings. We only had to change the `timezone` parameter, remember? In case something goes wrong, go back to the `zabbix.conf` file and check the parameters:

10. Next, we can fill in our connection details to connect to the database. If you remember, we did this already when we installed the server. Don't panic, it's completely normal. Zabbix, as we will see later, can be setup in a modular way so the frontend and the server both need to know where the database is and what the login credentials are. Press **Test connection** and when you get an **OK** just press **Next** again:

3. Configure DB connection

Please create database manually, and set the configuration parameters for connection to this database.

Press "Test connection" button when done.

Database type	MySQL ▼
Database host	localhost
Database port	0 0 - use default port
Database name	zabbix
User	zabbix
Password	••••••

OK

Test connection

« Previous   Next »

11. Next screen, we have to fill in some **Zabbix server details**. Host and port should already be filled in; if not, put the correct IP and port in the fields. The field **Name** is not really important for the working of our Zabbix server but it's probably better to fill in a meaningful name here for your Zabbix installation:

12. Now our setup is finished, and we can just click **Next** till we get our login screen. The **Username** and **Password** are standard the first time we set up the Zabbix server and are **Admin** for **Username** and **zabbix** for the **Password**:

How it works...

For the frontend, we had to install the web interface package from our Zabbix repository. For the web interface to work, we had to install a web server; one of the dependencies of Zabbix is the Apache web server. It is possible that in other repositories, this is not the case, so always make sure that Apache or some other web server is installed. The installed frontend is written in PHP.

To be able to connect to the web interface from another system, we had to open the firewall port on our Zabbix server, this was port 80.

Because the Zabbix setup can be modular, the frontend needs to know the location, the username and password of the database, and also the location of the Zabbix server and the correct port the Zabbix server communicates through. Normally, the standard port of the Zabbix server is 10051 and in our case everything is installed locally so localhost can be used.

If you make use of SELinux, you need to alter some of its settings or else, Zabbix will not work. Either you disable SELinux completely in the `/etc/selinux/config` file by replacing the `SELINUX=enforcing` parameter to `SELINUX=permissive` parameter. Once this is done, you run from the command line `setenforce 0`. Another option is to configure SELinux and this is the safest way. This can be done by running the following commands from the prompt:

```
setsebool -P zabbix_can_network on    (for the agent)

setsebool -P httpd_can_network_connect  on  (for the server)

setsebool -P httpd_can_network_connect_db  on (for the server)
```

There's more...

Of course there is more to the frontend that can be tweaked. In case we want to edit the frontend configuration, it can be done under the `/usr/share/zabbix/include/defines.inc.php` file.

Here is a list of the most important things that can be altered. A complete list can be found in the Zabbix online documentation.

`https://www.zabbix.com/documentation/2.4/manual/web_interface/definitions`.

Parameter	Option
ZBX_LOGIN_ATTEMPTS	Number of login attempts before ZBX_LOGIN_BLOCK is activated
ZBX_LOGIN_BLOCK	Number of seconds to wait after too many login attempts
ZBX_MIN_PERIOD	Min zoom period for graphs
ZBX_MAX_PERIOD	Max zoom period for graphs

Parameter	Option
ZBX_PERIOD_DEFAULT	Default graph period in seconds
GRAPH_YAXIS_SIDE_DEFAULT	Default side for the Y axis; can be changed from left to right
ZBX_WIDGET_ROWS	Popup row limit
ZBX_UNITS_ROUNDOFF_ THRESHOLD	Threshold value for roundoff constants
ZBX_UNITS_ROUNDOFF_ UPPER_LIMIT	Number of digits after comma, when value is greater than roundoff threshold
ZBX_UNITS_ROUNDOFF_ LOWER_LIMIT	Number of digits after comma, when value is less than roundoff threshold
ZBX_HISTORY_DATA_UPKEEP	Number of days, which will reflect on frontend choice when deciding which history or trends table to process

Installing Zabbix from source

We will now show you how to install Zabbix from source. Remember that for production, it's always better to install from the Zabbix repository or another repository such as **Extra Packages for Enterprise Linux** (**EPEL**). First of all, it will make your life easier when you want to upgrade but also when you want to remove some software. Maintainers of Zabbix packages in repositories such as EPEL are always in contact with Zabbix developers and improving the packages. If you compile it by yourself, chances are that you will miss something and will have to do it over later when your setup is already in production.

So why compile, you would think. Well if you can't wait for the latest and greatest new features then it can be a good thing to compile Zabbix in a test environment and try it out. Also, if you or some customer is in high need of one of the new features, it can be an option but then you really have to know what you are doing. Performance can also be a consideration.

> If you consider compiling from source, take a checklist with you that lists all options that you need.

Getting ready

To get started with our compilation, we need of course, an operating system and the Zabbix source code. In this case, I will show you how to compile on Red Hat or CentOS 6.x.

For our setup we will need a local working MySQL server with a working Zabbix database and a web server properly configured.

You can also look in the Zabbix online manual under **Installation | Installation from sources**. `https://www.zabbix.com/documentation/2.4/manual/installation/install`.

How to do it...

1. First we download the Zabbix source code which can be obtained from the Zabbix website. When going to download, click on **download again**; Zabbix stable source is the first on top. Save the file in the `/usr/src` folder.

2. Next thing of course, is the extraction of the `tar.gz` file we have downloaded. This can be done with `tar`. For example:

    ```
    # tar -zxvf zabbix-2.4.x.tar.gz
    ```

3. We now have a folder that contains the Zabbix source code. For example: the `/usr/src/zabbix-2.4.x` folder.

4. We need to install Apache, MySQL, PHP, and some other libraries for our server. This can be done with:

    ```
    # yum install httpd php php-mysql php-bcmath php-mbstring php-gd php-xml mysql mysql-server -y
    ```

Zabbix supports the following versions: MySQL 5.03 or higher, PostgreSQL 8.1 or higher, Apache 1.3.12 or higher, PHP 5.3 or higher. A full list can be found here:

`https://www.zabbix.com/documentation/2.4/manual/installation/requirements`.

5. We also need a user and a group for the Zabbix server to run as since we don't want to run our server as root. So we will create a group and a user Zabbix first:

    ```
    # groupadd zabbix
    ```

    ```
    # useradd -g zabbix zabbix
    ```

6. To be able to start the compilation process, we need to install some extra packages on our system before we can begin, of course:

    ```
    # yum install gcc mysql-devel libxml2-devel net-snmp-devel curl-devel unixODBC-devel OpenIPMI-devel libssh2-devel iksemel-devel openldap-devel
    ```

7. For some packages you probably have to add the EPEL repository to your setup. `https://fedoraproject.org/wiki/EPEL`.

8. To get a list of all options supported when compiling we have to run next command in the extracted folder:

```
# ./configure --help
```

9. To compile the sources for a Zabbix server, you could run something like the following line. Options depend on your installation:

```
# ./configure --enable-server --enable-agent --with-mysql --
enable-ipv6 --with-net-snmp --with-libcurl --with-libxml2 --
with-openipmi --with-unixodbc --with-ssh2 --with-ldap --with-
jabber
```

10. If finished correctly, you will get a message telling you to run 'make install' now. If you get an error, you probably have to install a missing development library. The last line will tell you what is missing:

```
# make install
```

11. The compiler will be running for sometime depending on the speed of your system; just let it run till it stops. It will stop after sometime and when there are no errors at the end, your Zabbix server will be compiled.

12. You need to configure database connection settings, and so on. just like we did with the installation from the Zabbix server from package. The standard location of the configuration files and the Zabbix server can be found under:

```
# /usr/local/etc/ → Zabbix configuration files
```

```
# /usr/local/sbin/ → Zabbix server
```

If you want to change the location of the Zabbix server installation you could make use of the `-prefix=/PATH` option when compiling.

If you have issues don't forget to disable SELinux or better still, put proper SELinux permissions.

The `-j` option can be used to speed up compiling when running `make` on a multicore computer such as `make -j 4`.

`http://stackoverflow.com/questions/414714/compiling-with-g-using-multiple-cores`.

13. As you probably have noticed, there are no init scripts when you compile from source. This is something you will have to create by yourself. Or you could use the ones provided by Zabbix. Those can be found under the `/usr/src/zabbix-2,4,x/misc/init.d` file.

14. Now we also need to install the Zabbix frontend. The most easiest way is to copy the files into a sub directory of the HTML root:

```
# mkdir /var/www/html/zabbix
# cd /usr/src/zabbix-2.4.x/frontends/php
# cp -a . /var/www/html/zabbix
# chown -R —no-dereference apache:apache /var/www/html/zabbix
```

15. Best is to create a `zabbix.conf` file for Apache in the `/etc/httpd/conf.d/` folder:

```
<Directory "/var/www/html/zabbix">
    Options FollowSymLinks
    AllowOverride None
    Order allow,deny
    Allow from all

    php_value max_execution_time 300
    php_value memory_limit 128M
    php_value post_max_size 16M
    php_value upload_max_filesize 2M
    php_value max_input_time 300
    php_value date.timezone Europe/Brussels
</Directory>
```

How it works...

The downloaded source code from Zabbix will be extracted first in a folder. To be able to run the Zabbix server as a standard user and not as root, we need to create a group and a user. In this case, we added a group `zabbix` and created a user `zabbix` and linked the user to the same group.

We then downloaded the development libraries and our gcc compiler so that we were able to compile the Zabbix server from the source code.

The same thing can be done for the Zabbix agent and the Zabbix proxy, except that only other compiling options are needed.

There's more...

Since Zabbix 2.2, there is the possibility to monitor virtual machines in VMware. For this to work, it is necessary to give the `--with-libxml2` option when compiling, else this functionality will not work.

When compiling an agent, we can make use of the same source code we have downloaded for the compilation of the Zabbix server. The only thing we need to do now, is launch.

```
# ./configure --enable-agent
```

When compiling fails, chances that you are missing some development libraries for one of the new options you have added are great. If you are not sure what option has caused this, then it can make sense to remove some options and start over. Later if compiling works, you can then add the new options again, one by one, to see where it fails. Zabbix also provides a URL with information on how to install from source:

```
https://www.zabbix.com/documentation/2.4/manual/installation/install.
```

Installing the server in a distributed setup

Next, we will see how to install the Zabbix server in a distributed way. This means that we will install all three components on different servers. In big setups, this can be a win as the frontend, Zabbix server, and database will have their own hardware.

Getting ready

For this setup to work, we need three machines, all with the latest version from Red Hat 6.x or CentOS 6.x with proper host name resolution, either by **Domain Name System** (**DNS**) or by host file. In this setup, I will talk about the setup of the server, db, and frontend. This time, we will disable SELinux on all machines as it is slightly more complicated and out of the scope of this book.

How to do it...

1. First thing to do is add on every host the Zabbix repository from Zabbix like we have done with our server installation. Remember the repository can be found in the Zabbix installation manual under installation from package.

2. On the DB server we install, of course, the MySQLserver:

   ```
   # yum install  mysql-server
   # service mysqld start
   # /usr/sbin/mysql_secure_installation (same options as before)
   # chkconfig mysqld on
   ```

3. Open the firewall on the database server and disable SELinux on all servers:

```
# iptables -I INPUT 5 -m state --state NEW -m tcp -p tcp --
dport 3306 -j ACCEPT
```

```
# iptables save
```

```
# service iptables restart
```

```
# vi /etc/selinux/config
```

4. Change the next value to `permissive`:

```
# SELINUX=permissive
```

5. Reboot the database server so that SELinux is disabled or type from the prompt:

```
# setenforce 0
```

6. Next thing we do is create our database and grant rights to it. When granting rights, don't forget to give rights to the Zabbix user from the Zabbix server as our connection is not alone from localhost but also from the server:

```
# mysql -u root -p
```

```
mysql> create database zabbix character set utf8 collate utf8_bin;
```

```
mysql> grant all privileges on zabbix.* to zabbix@localhost
identified by 'some_password';
```

```
mysql> grant all privileges on zabbix.* to zabbix@server-ip
identified by 'some_password';
```

```
mysql> grant all privileges on zabbix.* to zabbix@frontend-ip
identified by 'some_password';
```

```
mysql> exit
```

7. Next thing we have to do is upload the correct schemas for the Zabbix installation. For this, we have to copy the schemas from the Zabbix server or install the `zabbix-mysql-server` package:

```
# cd /usr/share/doc/zabbix-server-mysql-2.4.x/create
```

```
# mysql -uroot zabbix < schema.sql
```

```
# mysql -uroot zabbix < images.sql
```

```
# mysql -uroot zabbix < data.sql
```

8. Now on the server, install the Zabbix server:

```
# yum install zabbix-server zabbix-server-mysql
```

```
# chkconfig zabbix-server on
```

9. Edit the Zabbix server configuration file:

   ```
   # vi /etc/zabbix/zabbix_server.conf
   DBHost=<ip of the db>
   DBName=zabbix
   DBUser=zabbix
   DBPassword=<some password>
   #DBSocket=/var/lib/mysql/mysql.sock (put this in comment)
   DBPort=3306
   ```

10. Start the Zabbix server and check the log file if there are no errors logged:

    ```
    # service zabbix-server start
    # tail /var/log/zabbix/zabbix_server.log
    ```

11. Open port `10051` on the firewall:

    ```
    # iptables -I INPUT 5 -m state --state NEW -m tcp -p tcp --dport 10051 -j ACCEPT
    # iptables save
    # service iptables restart
    ```

12. Install the frontend on the server:

    ```
    # yum install zabbix-web-mysql
    # chkconfig httpd on
    ```

13. Uncomment the `timezone` value and replace `Riga` with your location:

    ```
    # vi /etc/httpd/conf.d/zabbix.conf
    php_value date.timezone Europe/Riga
    ```

14. Open port `80` on the firewall:

    ```
    # iptables -I INPUT 5 -m state --state NEW -m tcp -p tcp --dport 80 -j ACCEPT
    # iptables save
    # service iptables restart
    # service httpd start
    ```

15. Now let's open our browser and go to the frontend server:

    ```
    # http://frontend/zabbix
    ```

After the first screens with the **PHP** option check if we get our screen with the connection settings for the database. Fill in the name or IP of our DB server with the DB name, username, and password:

Test the connection to the database, in case of problems, you could try to connect from the shell:

```
# mysql -h <db ip> -u<username> -p<password> <db name>
```

Or try to telnet

```
# telnet <db ip> <port>   EX: telnet 192.168.1.5 3306
```

When the connection tests are fine you can just click **Next**. This will bring us to the connection screen of the server as you can see in next screenshot.

16. In the location of hostname, we have to fill in the hostname of our Zabbix server. The port is the port the server uses for the communication. Remember we have opened it in our firewall before? The port `10051` is the standard port but can be changed in the `zabbix_server.conf` file in case you want to change this:

For the name, we can give anything that makes sense for our setup. Now when we click **Next**, our Zabbix server is up and running and we can log in with the standard login and password: **Admin / zabbix**.

How it works...

Our Zabbix server, database and frontend are all installed on different servers. Because the database needs to be able to communicate with our server we had to open port 3306 in our firewall and grant the permissions, so that the server and frontend had rights to connect to our database.

The Zabbix server communicates on port 10051, so for the server, we had to open this port in the firewall on the Zabbix server.

Our frontend needs a web server so Apache was installed automatically when we installed the Zabbix package. To be able to see the Zabbix frontend, we had to open port 80 in the firewall.

As the frontend is not aware that we have installed a distributed setup we had to tell the frontend that our database was installed on another location and the same was done for the Zabbix server:

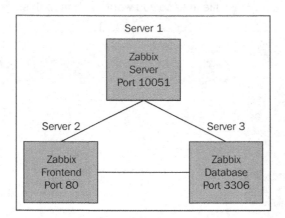

There's more...

For the port of the database we did not put in 3306 port but 0. This way Zabbix knows that we have used the standard port. In case you changed it in your setup, you have to add the correct port instead of 0.

In case you edit the /etc/httpd/conf.d/zabbix.conf configuration file instead of making changes from the web interface, make sure that you don't remove the 0. If the port is empty, the configuration will not work.

Another issue occurs if Zabbix itself is down. Some companies make use of a small extra Zabbix server that monitors the Zabbix server. This is an easy, not too expensive option.

The setup of Zabbix as a virtual machine is also an option. Just make sure that the database in that case is on dedicated storage as a virtualized database on shared storage is not a good idea.

Yet another solution could be to build a cluster. The Zabbix server itself does not support a cluster setup but it can be done manually. There are several guides on how to do this available on the www.zabbix.org webpage.

2
Getting Around in Zabbix

In this chapter we will cover the following topics:

- Exploring the frontend
- Zabbix definitions
- Acknowledging triggers
- Zabbix architecture
- Getting an overview of the latest data

Introduction

In this chapter, we will talk about how the Zabbix frontend works and where to find the most important things in the interface and all the things that set Zabbix apart from the others. We will explain how to acknowledge problems from triggers that were activated when problems were detected. We will see how we can customize the frontend to our needs and explain the definitions being used in Zabbix. Next, we will show you how the Zabbix architecture is set up, so that you have a better understanding of where to look when things go wrong. Towards the end of the chapter, we will show you how to get an easy overview of the latest data in Zabbix.

Exploring the frontend

It's now time to start exploring the web interface. The web interface is not very straightforward, and you may find it difficult to get around. In this recipe, we will guide you through the Zabbix frontend, so that you can easily find your way in the Zabbix web interface.

Getting ready

In this recipe, we start with the standard Zabbix configuration. So you need a basic CentOS or RHEL setup or another Linux OS with Zabbix properly set up. If you haven't set up Zabbix yet, you have to do this first. If you don't know or have forgotten how to install Zabbix, return back to *Chapter 1, Zabbix Configuration* or have a look at the Zabbix documentation at `http://www.zabbix.com/documentation.php`. Select your Zabbix version currently still version 2.4. For installation instructions go to **Zabbix Manual | 3 Installation**.

How to do it...

As you can see in the following image, the first page that we get when we log in is the main page, with an overview of the information received from Zabbix. This is your personal dashboard that can be customized to your own needs and preferences. All boxes on this screen that you see, such as **Status of Zabbix**, **System status**, and so on. are drag-and-drop based. On top, you will see two menu bars. First menu bar starts with **Monitoring** and the bar below starts with **Dashboard**. Move your mouse to **Configuration** without clicking, then select **hosts** from the menu bar below **Configuration**. As you may have noticed, we can move around in the Zabbix menu without clicking on the menu bar. We only have to click on **hosts** if we want to go to hosts in the menu.

The first menu bar is the main bar where we split up things in Zabbix such as **Configuration**, **Inventory**, **Reports**, and so on. As we will see later, depending on what permissions you have, you will see more or less from this menu bar. The second bar will show you the options for each item you have selected in the first menu section.

Just below the bar that starts with Dashboard, you will see **History**. **History** will show you the history of places you have been in the Zabbix frontend. This makes it easier to go back to a page you have been before.

At the bottom of the web page, you will see the version of the Zabbix frontend. In this case you will see Zabbix 2.4.x on the bottom of the screenshot:

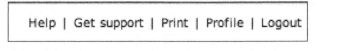

ZABBIX

Monitoring | Inventory | Reports | Configuration | Administration

Dashboard | Overview | Web | Latest data | Triggers | Events | Graphs | Screens | Maps | Discovery | IT services

History: Dashboard

PERSONAL DASHBOARD

Favourite graphs

No graphs added.

Graphs »

Favourite screens

No screens added.

Screens »   Slide shows »

Favourite maps

No maps added.

Maps »

Status of Zabbix

Parameter	Value	Details
Zabbix server is running	Yes	localhost:10051
Number of hosts (enabled/disabled/templates)	39	0 / 1 / 38
Number of items (enabled/disabled/not supported)	0	0 / 0 / 0
Number of triggers (enabled/disabled [problem/ok])	0	0 / 0 [0 / 0]
Number of users (online)	2	1
Required server performance, new values per second	0	-

Updated: 18:59:16

System status

Host group	Disaster	High	Average	Warning	Information	Not classified
No host groups found.						

Updated: 18:59:15

The first menu that we will discuss is the upper right menu. This menu has some handy features for the system and some user-only settings:

Help | Get support | Print | Profile | Logout

1. The first option **Help** brings us to the Zabbix documentation page. This is an easy shortcut if you need some help with the configuration of Zabbix.

2. The **Get support** link will redirect you to the Zabbix page where all different options of technical support are explained. Remember that Zabbix is a 100 percent free product. So one of the ways Zabbix can make money and develop our nice free monitoring solution is by selling support.

3. **Print** will make your life easier when you want to print the Zabbix page on paper. It will take away the menu from the top, so that only relevant information on the web page is left to print.

4.   The next option **Profile** is unique for each user.

❑   In the first tab **User,** we can alter our password, interface language, and the preferred theme that we want to use. If some language is missing, it is possible that you need to install the locales on your server. There is also an option to **Auto-login** without username or password. An **Auto-logout** function that will make sure no one enters the system when you forget to logout or lock your computer. The **Refresh** option let's you set the number of seconds after which the information on the page is refreshed. The **Rows per page** option will let you decide how many rows are shown but remember less rows means faster loading. **URL (after login)** is the web page you will see after the login.

URL (after login) can be handy for a service center to see a page with screens or sideshows after they have logged in. Be careful; this will not work for guest users as they do not have to login.

USER PROFILE: Zabbix Administrator

| User | Media | Messaging |

Password	Change password
Language	English (en_GB) ⬍
Theme	System default ⬍
Auto-login	☑
Auto-logout (min 90 seconds)	☐ 900
Refresh (in seconds)	30
Rows per page	50
URL (after login)	

Save   Cancel

❑   The **Media** tab is the place where the user can add the media that he or she wants to use to get notifications. Zabbix allows at this time, the use of **Email**, Jabber, and/or SMS. The user can decide here which media is active for hours and days. Also, the severity level for getting notifications can be chosen here:

New media

Type	Email ⬍
Send to	
When active	1-7,00:00-24:00
Use if severity	☑ Not classified
	☑ Information
	☑ Warning
	☑ Average
	☑ High
	☑ Disaster
Status	Enabled ⬍

Add Cancel

❑ Next and last tab is the **Messaging** tab. Here each individual user can set his or her own notifications for the desktop. This means that each user can be notified by a popup on the desktop with a sound. Select **Frontend messaging** to get notified. Select the timeout period (how long the message stays on the screen) and select if you would like to get notified once every 10 seconds or if you would like to keep sound repeated while the message is on screen. Next thing to do is select for each **Trigger severity** if we want to be notified and what sound we want to hear.

> This setting is for each user to be set individually and cannot be overruled by admin. This can be annoying in a big room like a service desk where everybody has his or her own notification sounds.

User	Media	**Messaging**			

Frontend messaging	☐				
Message timeout (seconds)	60				
Play sound	Once ⬍				
Trigger severity	☑ Recovery	alarm_ok ⬍	Play	Stop	
	☑ Not classified	no_sound ⬍	Play	Stop	
	☑ Information	alarm_information ⬍	Play	Stop	
	☑ Warning	alarm_warning ⬍	Play	Stop	
	☑ Average	alarm_average ⬍	Play	Stop	
	☑ High	alarm_high ⬍	Play	Stop	
	☑ Disaster	alarm_disaster ⬍	Play	Stop	

Save Cancel

5. Back to our previous menu, we have the logout option left. This one explains itself; we use it to log out after a hard day at work. More information can be found in the Zabbix documentation under **Web interface | User profile** or for Zabbix 2.4 follow next URL: `https://www.zabbix.com/documentation/2.4/manual/web_interface/user_profile`. Back to our front page, we have our next important menu in Zabbix. This menu is probably the menu you will use the most be it as normal user or as admin user. We will explain you what each button in the menu bar does, so that you get a good understanding of the items in the Zabbix menu:

6. The first row shows us the option **Monitoring**. When we put our mouse over **Monitoring**, the bar below will adapt and show everything that we need to get our data that was gathered by Zabbix visualized. This can be raw data that we see or a graph, map, slideshow, and so on.

7. The next button named **Inventory** will bring us to the inventory system of Zabbix. Zabbix can make an inventory of a park that we monitor and when we go to inventory, we will get an overview of each host inventory data by parameter or the complete host inventory details.

8. When going to **Reports** we will get an overview of some standard predefined and user customizable reports. Reports will show us the the **Status of Zabbix**, **Availability report**, **Triggers top 100**, and **Bar report**.

9. The next item is **Configuration**. The **Configuration** menu contains a list of options to choose from, all with focus on configuring Zabbix. It contains configuration settings such as **hosts**, **host groups**, **templates**, **actions**, **maps**, and so on. This menu option is the most important when configuring Zabbix. Only administrators and super administrators will be able to see this option.

10. And the last menu **Administration** is for the administrative functions of Zabbix such as the creation of users, media types, authentication, and so on. In Zabbix, we logged in as the admin user. This user is a super administrator and only super administrators will be able to see this option.

11. On the top right of our web page, we have a global **Search** box in Zabbix. This box allows us to do a search for host, host groups and templates in Zabbix and the entities that belong to them.

12. Just below the **Search** box we have another button that looks like a working tool. This acts as a configurable filter. Click on it and you will see that you have the possibility to enable the dashboard filter and adjust some settings like only show certain host groups or only certain levels of severity and even only unacknowledged problems.

13. The next button that looks like a square with 4 arrows in it is to put our Zabbix page in full screen mode. This can be handy for people working in a service center or just to avoid getting distracted with all menu options:

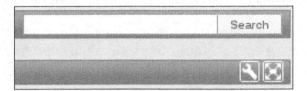

Zabbix will give users access to parts of the menu based on the user role. Besides super administrators there are also administrators in Zabbix. Administrators will see everything except the **Administration** menu. Normal users will see everything except **Configuration** and **Administration** in the menu.

14. Next on our front page, are some columns with all kind of statuses from Zabbix such as the **Status of Zabbix**, **System status**, and also some columns with favorites. Let me go a little deeper into what their use is and why you should care about them.

15. Probably one of the more important tables is the **Status of Zabbix** table. The first line will show us if the Zabbix server is running. Remember that the frontend is a different package, so the fact that we can login to the web interface does not mean that our Zabbix server is running. Here we can see with a **Yes** or a **No** if the server is running and if the Zabbix server runs local or on another server. Next line will show us the **Number of hosts** that are configured and behind it the number of hosts being monitored, not monitored and the number of templates.

16. Next line will show us the **Number of items** that are linked to hosts that are enabled in Zabbix. Behind this column we see the number of items that are active being monitored, those that are disabled and at last, the ones that are not supported. Be careful with unsupported items, as Zabbix will check them from time to time to see if data can be gathered from them so they will eat up your resources.

17. Next, we see **Number of triggers**. First number will show us the total number of triggers linked to enabled hosts. In the next column, we see the number of enabled and disabled triggers and then two numbers between square brackets. First number will show us the number of triggers in **problem** state and then those in **ok** state.

18. The next line tells us the **Number of users** configured in Zabbix. Beware, only the last column will show us the value of users online in Zabbix. Zabbix comes standard with guest user activated so this is the second user.

19. The last line will show us the **Required server performance**. This number will tell us how many new values per second Zabbix expects. This number is an indication of how many values per second will go into our database and can be a good indication to see what kind of hardware we need. You could compare it with others on the internet.

Status of Zabbix		
Parameter	**Value**	**Details**
Zabbix server is running	Yes	localhost:10051
Number of hosts (monitored/not monitored/templates)	39	0 / 1 / 38
Number of items (monitored/disabled/not supported)	0	0 / 0 / 0
Number of triggers (enabled/disabled) [problem/ok]	0	0 / 0 [0 / 0]
Number of users (online)	2	1
Required server performance, new values per second	0	-
Updated: 20:45:16		

> This status can also be found in the menu bar under **Reports | Status of zabbix**.

20. Our next dashboard widget is the **System status** widget. In this place we get an overview of all host groups and the status of the servers in the group. If one of the servers in one of the groups gets a problem, the color will change from green to something else. When we hover with the mouse over the box with a new color, a message is shown and tells us which server has a problem:

System status						
Host group	**Disaster**	**High**	**Average**	**Warning**	**Information**	**Not classified**
Zabbix servers	0	0	0	0	0	0
Updated: 21:27:26						

21. Just below system status, we have the **Host status** widget. Here we get an overview of our hosts with a quick indication of how many problems there are on our host. When we hover over without the mouse, we will see how many of our problems are critical, average, and so on:

Host status			
Host group	Without problems	With problems	Total
Zabbix servers	0	1	1
Updated: 21:35:27			

22. The **Last 20 issues** widget is an overview of the last 20 issues that have been detected by Zabbix. It will show you the time the last status change happened and also how many minutes ago this was, so you have the opportunity to acknowledge the problem. When you acknowledge a problem, you get a box where you can write what you have done to solve the issue or some other information:

Last 20 issues						
Host	Issue	Last change	Age	Info	Ack	Actions
Zabbix server	Zabbix agent on Zabbix server is unreachable for 5 minutes	11 Jul 2014 21:33:00	6m 27s		No	
					1 of 1 issue is shown	
Updated: 21:39:27						

23. The last box at the bottom of our page is the **Web monitoring** widget. It is possible to monitor web pages with Zabbix. This widget will show us an overview of the websites we monitor per group and how many are in status **Ok** or **Failed**.

Web monitoring			
Host group	Ok	Failed	Unknown
websites	1	0	0
Updated: 22:14:00			

24. On our left side of the web page are some small boxes with favorites for graphs, screens and maps. As the name suggests, here each user can add his favorite links to graphs, screens, and maps in Zabbix:

25. As you may already have noticed, there are two buttons on every widget in the top right corner. The first context menu will allow us to change the refresh list in case of the monitoring applets in the middle of our screen. On the left side with the favorite widgets, it will allow us to quickly add some favorites.

The second context button will make it possible to close our widget in case we are not interested in the information from it.

It is possible to drag and drop all widgets on the screen to another location on the screen; this way you can change the place they show up to maximize the full potential of the size from the screen or monitor you are working on.

How it works...

We have seen that the Zabbix dashboard can be built dynamically. We can move widgets around so that we do not have to scroll around in our screen to find the information we need. The first menu bar on top where we can choose from monitoring, inventory, reports, configuration, and administration is the most important menu. For each category we hover over, it will show the options available in the menu bar below it. Also depending on what rights the user has, this menu bar will show more or less.

See also

▶ In the *Creating users* recipe in *Chapter 3*, we will explain how to create users with the correct rights.

Zabbix definitions

In the previous topic where we explained the frontend, we already talked a bit about hosts, triggers, items, and so on. So I am sure you have a lot of questions about what they are. Before we move on with our Zabbix book, I will first explain you a bit about the Zabbix definitions so that you have an idea what everything is.

Getting ready

By now you should have an up and running Zabbix configuration and you should know your way around the frontend. If you have no clue how the frontend works, then go back to previous topic and have a look at *Exploring the frontend*.

How to do it...

In Zabbix we call hosts, devices that we want to monitor. Of course, those devices need a network connection so that our Zabbix server can talk to them.

Hosts can be added in Zabbix under **Configuration | Hosts**.

1. When we have hosts, it makes sense to group them together based on certain common unique aspects they have, for instance, all Linux or all Windows servers. Groups in Zabbix can contain hosts and templates and are being used to assign access rights to hosts for different user groups. Host groups can be found under **Configuration | Host groups**.

2. Now that we have hosts and host groups, we want to monitor certain things such as memory, CPU load, network interfaces, and so on. This, we call in Zabbix Items. Items can be added on host level or on template level. Preferred way is of course, on template level as we can make use of templates as many times as we want. Items can be found under **Configuration | Hosts | Items** or **Configuration | Templates | Items**.

3. If we want to monitor hosts, we could create checks for each host or make use of Zabbix templates. Templates are a set of entities such as items, triggers, screens, and so on, put together ready to be applied to one or more hosts. Advantage is that we save time when configuring or making mass changes. Templates can be found under **Configuration | Templates**.

4. Now that we have our items in Zabbix, it makes sense to put certain thresholds that we don't want to pass, for example, CPU load higher than 5 or memory lower than 256 MB. In Zabbix, we make use of triggers to define our thresholds. Triggers are logical expressions that evaluate the data of our items and put an item in a state of **ok** or **problem**. Triggers can be found just like items on host level or on template level under **Configuration | Hosts | Triggers** or **Configuration | Templates | Triggers**.

5. When a trigger changes its state, an event will be generated in Zabbix. Other things in Zabbix that generate events are auto-registration of agents and autodiscovery of network devices. Events can be found under **Monitoring | Events**.

6. Sometimes in Zabbix, we want certain actions to happen based on our events. An action consists of an operation (example: send an email) and a condition (example: when a trigger is in problem state). Actions can be found in the menu under **Configuration | Actions**.

7. Sometimes, sending an email to one person is not enough. It so happens that we want to notify more than one person in a certain sequence. For this, we have **escalations**. Back to **Configuration | Actions** under the tab **Operations** we can add all steps of different escalations we want to follow. Escalations are custom scenarios in an action. For instance, in one action we can send an email and then after 10 minutes send a text message to someone else. There is no limit in the number of escalations steps.

8. Media in Zabbix is used to define the way in which we will get our notifications delivered. Remember that media is user dependent and can be found under **Profile | Media** but also under **Administration | Media types**. Here we list all media types allowed with their proper configuration.

9. Notifications is what we use in Zabbix to notify someone about some event that happened by making use of the selected media channel from the user. Under **Administration | Notifications**, we can see who was notified at what time by what media.

10. Sometimes the options that Zabbix gives us are not enough. For cases like this, Zabbix allows us to extend Zabbix with remote commands. Remote commands are predefined commands that execute automatically on a monitored host under certain conditions. Those can be found under **Administration | Scripts**.

11. When we monitor several network items in Zabbix, it makes sense to put them in a group. This way, it will be easier later to check all data about those items. For this, Zabbix uses applications. When we create items, we can select applications for our items. Applications can be found under **Configuration | Hosts | Applications** or **Configuration | Templates | Applications**.

12. In Zabbix it is possible to monitor web services. We can build advanced scenarios to check our websites. This we call **Web scenarios** and can be found under **Configuration | Host | Web** or **Configuration | Template | Web**.

13. The frontend as we have seen earlier is the web interface from Zabbix.

14. When we want to extend our Zabbix monitoring solution, we can do this by making use of the **Zabbix API**. The API makes use of the JSON **Remote Procedure Call** (**RPC**) protocol and can create/update/fetch objects such as hosts, templates, groups, and so on.

15. Our environment makes use of a **Zabbix server**. The Zabbix server is a software process that performs monitoring. It interacts with our agents and proxies, makes calculations, sends notifications and stores all data in a central database.

16. The **Zabbix agent** is the piece of software that we install on our hosts to monitor local resources and applications.

17. Nodes are like proxies but with a full server configuration, set up in a hierarchical way. Nodes are deprecated and are removed in Zabbix 2.4, so we can forget about them. Before Zabbix 2.4, we had **DM** under **Administration** which is now renamed as **Proxies**.

How it works...

The definitions in Zabbix are things you should learn before you really start working with Zabbix as we will be using them throughout the book. It is crucial to know, that when we talk about a host, it can be just any device connected to a network which we want to monitor (example: switches, temperature sensors, gateways, door sensors, printers, and so on). Just as it is important to know what hosts are, it is important to know when we want to monitor something like **CPU iowait** or the state of a network device. For this, we need to create **Items** on the host. And that it is best done by creating items on templates and then link a template with one or more hosts. Another thing we have seen is that we have to put certain thresholds on the items that we monitor to get notified about certain problems. This we call **Triggers** and just like items, we should place them in a template, so that we don't have to create the same trigger over and over.

As always, it's a good idea to check the **Zabbix documentation** for the latest update about the definitions:

```
https://www.zabbix.com/documentation/2.4/manual/concepts/definitions.
```

Acknowledging triggers

In this recipe we will see how to acknowledge triggers when they happen. Why do you need to know? To save others the frustration of looking into a problem that has already been resolved by you.

Getting ready

To be able to acknowledge some triggers, you need a complete functional Zabbix installation. To acknowledge some trigger, you need a failure on one of the triggers. If no trigger is in alarm then you could try for example, to increase the CPU load or stop the service from the Zabbix client.

How to do it...

When we go in Zabbix to our web interface, we have a list with the last 20 issues. As you can see, we have multiple columns with one being the **Last change**.

1. This column is the date and time when the item had its last status change. The next column **Age** will tell us how long the problem is already there.

2. The **Ack** column will allow us to acknowledge the problem. This way we can work in an organized way with multiple people in Zabbix:

Last 20 issues							
Host	**Issue**		**Last change**	**Age**	**Info**	**Ack**	**Actions**
Zabbix server	Zabbix agent on Zabbix server is unreachable for 5 minutes		11 Jul 2014 21:33:00	16d 20h 59m	?	No	
						1 of 1 issue is shown	
Updated: 18:32:03							

3. When we click on the **Ack** button, we are able to type some information in the message box. This can be a small text explaining what has been done to fix the problem:

Acknowledge alarm by "Admin (Zabbix Administrator)"	
Message	
	Acknowledge and return · Acknowledge · Cancel

 Acknowledgment status can also be used when defining an action operation. For example, we can send a text message to the direct manager if a technician hasn't acknowledged the problem for a certain amount of time.

How it works...

So how does it work? Based on our items that we have created and the triggers that were set on those items, an event will be generated in Zabbix. Those events are used to create actions but those events can also be acknowledged to notify other users that we have fixed the problem or that we are busy with the problem. This we can write down in our message box.

Acknowledgments can be done from the front page from the **20 Last item** box or we can go in the Zabbix menu to **Monitoring | Events** and acknowledge the status of our item.

Zabbix architecture

The Zabbix architecture is as we have seen before dynamic. We can create a setup where everything is in one server or we can split up the server in three different servers. One for the database, another one for the frontend and another server for the Zabbix server.

When our infrastructure grows, we would probably want to add some proxies to offload the Zabbix server or maybe, we need to pass a firewall. We will now see some solutions that are possible with Zabbix.

Getting ready

If you would like to test this setup, you will need some servers to install the database, frontend, and Zabbix server like we have seen before in *Chapter 1, Zabbix Configuration*, but also an extra server to install a Zabbix proxy.

How to do it...

The most basic setup in Zabbix is the setup we did in chapter one, with all the Zabbix components installed on one server:

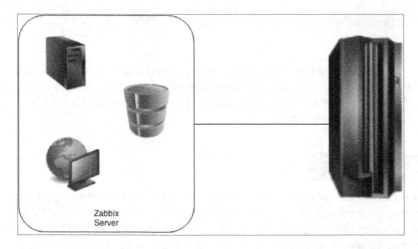

Zabbix
Server

From the server we monitor the hosts in our company. The advantage is that this setup is easy to set up as we don't have to configure multiple servers and just connect to the hosts in our network. This setup is perfect for smaller companies where one hardware box can run the complete Zabbix server and where we don't have to worry about firewalls.

The problem with this setup is that once our Zabbix server gets bigger and when more and more users connect to the Zabbix web interface, it can get too slow. Splitting up the Zabbix server, database, and frontend on different hardware can solve our problem as the database will have its own dedicated hardware, and the web server has its own server to run on. This setup can be seen in the following figure:

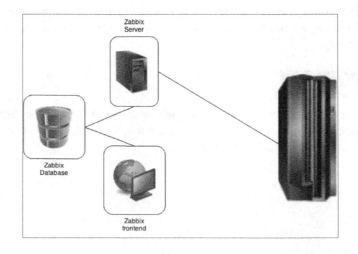

Zabbix
Server

Zabbix
Database

Zabbix
frontend

The problem with this setup is that in real life, we probably have some of our severs behind a firewall or on other locations or sometimes, we have so many servers that we have to invest in more powerful hardware for our Zabbix server. Also, sometimes we want to keep some servers in **Demilitarized Zone** (**DMZ**) and then we have to create holes in our firewall to let the Zabbix agents talk to the Zabbix server. This is not something we want to do for each host we want to monitor. In the following figure, we will show you the problem with a firewall and multiple hosts that we like to monitor.

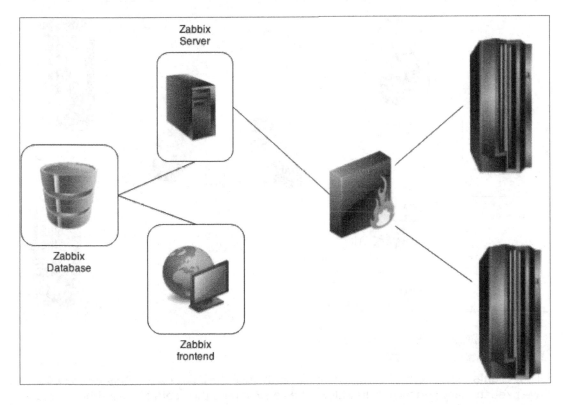

To solve this problem with our firewall, we can add a proxy to our setup. By adding a proxy, all clients can communicate with the proxy and the proxy can send all the data to the Zabbix server. This way, we only need to be sure that the Zabbix proxy can communicate to our Zabbix server through the firewall.

As an extra bonus, the Zabbix proxy will offload our Zabbix server as the proxy will do all the work (example: SMTP, SSH, IPMI checks). The proxy will also send all data at once to the Zabbix server, but the Zabbix server will still have to process all the data. Also when the communication goes down between proxy and Zabbix server, the Zabbix proxy can cache our data for one hour up to 30 days. This can be configured in the `zabbix_proxy.conf` file with the `ProxyLocalBuffer` parameter. This setup can be seen in the following figure:

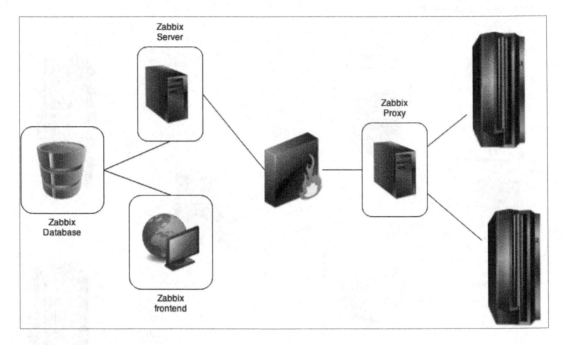

How it works...

All our clients will be configured to communicate through the Zabbix proxy. This way we don't have to open many ports in our firewall to let all agents pass their data to the Zabbix server. The Zabbix proxy runs with its own database. This can be the same or another database as the Zabbix server. Because we keep all data in a database on our Zabbix proxy, the data stays in the proxy for some time making it also perfect for installations where we have to send data over unstable networks.

We will configure the proxy to send all data through the firewall to our Zabbix server. The Zabbix server itself can be similar to what we have seen in *Chapter 1, Zabbix Configuration* a server with all components installed on it or it can be split up in three parts with the frontend, database, and Zabbix server installed on different hardware.

> Local sockets are faster then sending data over TCP/IP; so be sure when you split up your database on different hardware, that it will actually be faster.

Getting an overview of the latest data

This page is the Zabbix page where we can get an overview of all the data that we have been monitoring with our Zabbix server. After all, we want to know if we have received any values, isn't it ?

Getting ready

To be able to check anything on this page we need to have a running Zabbix setup with a host that has some active items on it already. It would be great if the item is also configured properly so that we can see the values that we have received.

How to do it...

In our Zabbix frontpage, go to **Monitoring | Latest Data**, this page will give you an overview of all the latest data that was gathered by Zabbix.

1. First thing we have to do is select the group and or the server where we want to see the latest data from. This can be done by typing the names in the correct fields or by clicking the **Select** button for each field. When you type in a field, Zabbix will try to guess the correct name. When you are ready, press **Filter**:

LATEST DATA					
Items					
			Hide filter		
Host groups:	type here to search	Select		Name:	
Hosts:	puppet3 X	Select	Show items without data:	☐	
Application:		Select	Show details:	☐	
		Filter Reset			

2. Once we have selected the correct server or group where we want to get our latest data from, we get to see depending on how many items we have created a lot of data on our screen:

Name ↑	Last check	Last value
CPU (13 Items)		
Context switches per second	-	-
CPU idle time	2015-01-12 19:22:19	81.47 %
CPU interrupt time	2015-01-12 19:22:20	0.2 %
CPU iowait time	2015-01-12 19:22:21	8.24 %
CPU nice time	2015-01-12 19:22:22	0 %
CPU softirq time	2015-01-12 19:22:23	0.08 %
CPU steal time	2015-01-12 19:22:24	0 %
CPU system time	2015-01-12 19:22:25	1.11 %
CPU user time	2015-01-12 19:22:26	8.39 %
Interrupts per second	-	-
Processor load (1 min average per core)	2015-01-12 19:22:16	0.08
Processor load (5 min average per core)	2015-01-12 19:22:17	0.04
Processor load (15 min average per core)	2015-01-12 19:22:15	0.04
General (5 Items)		
Memory (5 Items)		
OS (8 Items)		
Performance (13 Items)		
Processes (2 Items)		
Security (2 Items)		

3. The first column will show us a list with names. Those are the names from the application that we linked to our items. So when we click on it, we will get a list of all items related to that application.

4. In the next column **Last check,** we will see when was the last time our item was checked by Zabbix.

5. The next column **Last value** tells us what was the latest value Zabbix has received from our item.

6. The column **Change** will show us how much the value was changed since the previous check. This value can be either positive or negative. If you see no value at all and only a -, it means that the data was not changed since the last check.

7. If you are missing an item in the list, it probably means that Zabbix has no data yet. You can check this by clicking on the filter on top and selecting the **Show items without data** option in the filter. Then click on the **Filter** button and normally your item will pop up in the list with the column with **Last value,** being without value for this item.

8. Our last column will show us a graph or the history from our item. This way we can easily see how our item has behaved over a specific period in time.

How it works...

The latest data page will show you the latest data that Zabbix has received for each item that we have created. It will also show us what the difference was with the previous value from that item and we also have a link to watch a graph from the data of that item.

There is more ...

Since version 2.2.4, this page only shows the latest data of the last 24 hours. This limitation was introduced to keep load times lower of this page. The value can be changed if you like in the `/usr/share/zabbix/include/defines.inc.php` file. Here you can change the value of the `ZBX_HISTORY_PERIOD` parameter to something else in seconds.

If you are running one of the first 2.2 releases, it is possible that the latest data page only refreshes the values instead of the whole page. This feature was introduced with 2.2 to reduce load but had in some cases, the opposite effect. So best is that you upgrade to the latest version of Zabbix.

3
Groups, Users, and Permissions

In this chapter we will cover the following topics:

1. Creating hosts
2. Creating host groups
3. Creating users
4. Creating user groups
5. General administration
6. Authenticating users

Introduction

Now that we have seen how to install Zabbix and how to find our way around Zabbix, we will have a look at how to create hosts, add them to existing groups and create new groups. We will also have a look at the user permissions in Zabbix, as some changes have been introduced since Zabbix 2.2, and of course, all the different authentication methods available in Zabbix.

Creating hosts

The first thing that we will do is create some new hosts in Zabbix. To brush up your memory, hosts are devices that are connected to our network which need regular monitoring.

Getting ready...

To get started and add some hosts to our system, we need our Zabbix server up and running with a standard admin account; we will login with this admin account in order to create hosts. It's also useful if you understand the definitions in Zabbix, if you need to go over them again, return to the *Zabbix definitions* section of *Chapter 2*, for a quick revision of the same.

How to do it...

1. Let's start by logging into our frontend with the admin, super administrator or a different admin account in Zabbix.

2. In the menu, go to **Configuration | Hosts** and click in the upper right corner on **Create host** or click on the hostname of an existing host to edit one:

The **Host** tab contains the basic settings that we need to configure our host. The first box is **Host name** here we need to use a unique name. We need to use this hostname in our `zabbix_agentd.conf` agent configuration file for our active checks to work.

3. **Visible name** is a name that we can but do not have to give to our host. We can use it in case the real hostname is not really easy to remember. When we set the **Visible name**, this name will be the only visible name in screens, maps, filters, and so on.

4. From **Groups**, we select from the column **Other groups** the group to which our host belongs. A host must belong to at least one group. In the field **New group**, we can add a new group if the group that we want to use is not available yet. The host will then be added immediately to this new group.

5. Next we have a list of all kinds of interfaces such as agent interface, **Java Management Extensions (JMX)**, **Intelligent Platform Management Interface (IPMI)**, and **Simple Network Management Protocol (SNMP)**. Here we need to give for each interface that we want to use the correct IP address or DNS name. Next we fill in the correct port that we want to use for the interface.

6. With the **Add** button, we are able to add extra interfaces to our host. We will need it in case we have multiple network cards to choose from. With the **Remove** button, we can remove an interface again. If the **Remove** button in grayed out, it means that the interface is still active in an item.

7. Our host can be monitored by one of the Zabbix proxies or by the Zabbix server itself. When we want it to be monitored by a proxy, we select the correct proxy from the list **Monitored by proxy**.

8. From the **Status** button, we are able to choose **Monitored** and **Not Monitored**. When **Not Monitored** is chosen, our host will be disabled and won't be monitored.

It is also possible to make use of the **Clone** and **Full clone** buttons at the bottom of the host page to create a new host. When we click on clone all templates linked to our host will be kept on our cloned host. Full clone on the other hand will also clone directly attached entities applications, triggers, items, and so on.

9. From the **Templates** tab we are able to choose a template and link it to our host. To add a template, we just type in the name in the **Link new templates** box. We then press **Add**. We can now add another template the same way or click **Save** to save our settings:

| Host | Templates | IPMI | Macros | Host inventory |

Linked templates	Name	Action
	No templates linked.	

Link new templates	type here to search	Select
	Add	

Save | Clone | Full clone | Delete | Cancel

10. When we link our host with a template, the host will inherit all items, triggers, graphs and so on, from the template.

11. The **IPMI** tab will bring us to the window with the settings for our IPMI connection:

| Host | Templates | IPMI | Macros | Host inventory |

Authentication algorithm
- Default
- None
- MD2
- MD5
- Straight
- OEM
- RMCP+

Privilege level
- Callback
- User
- Operator
- Admin
- OEM

Username [   ]

Password [   ]

[Save] [Clone] [Full clone] [Delete] [Cancel]

12. In the box **Authentication algorithm**, we select the correct authentication algorithm for our **IPMI** interface. Next, we select the correct **Privilege level** for our user and finally we put the **Username** and **Password** for our user to log in to the **IPMI** interface.

13. The next tab **Macros**, allows us to set some host-level user macros. In the first column **Macro** we put our macro {$SOME-NAME} and in the **Value** field we put the value we want to give to our macro. Example: **Macro** {$COMMUNITY} with **Value**: public to define the community string for our switch:

| Host | Templates | IPMI | Macros | Host inventory |

Macro   **Value**

[{$MACRO}] ⇒ [value]   Remove

Add

[Save] [Clone] [Full clone] [Delete] [Cancel]

14. Our next and last tab **Host inventory** can be used to check the inventory of our host. The host inventory can be in the **Disabled** state if you don't like to use it; else we can put it in the **Manual** or **Automatic** state. Manual means that we fill in all the fields by hand. If we want to have an automated inventory system, we have to set the host inventory on **Automatic**. Based on the item that we create, we can select the inventory field in each item. Data will then be populated automatically.

> Some items that are especially useful when making use of the automated inventory solution are:
>
> `system.hw.chassis[full|type|vendor|model|serial]`: Root permissions needed
>
> `system.hw.cpu[all|cpunum,full|maxfreq|vendor|model|cur fr eq]`
>
> `system.hw.devices[pci|usb]`
>
> `system.hw.macaddr[interface,short|full]`
>
> `system.sw.arch`
>
> `system.sw.os[name|short|full]`
>
> `system.sw.packages[package,manager,short|full]`.

How it works...

When we want to monitor our infrastructure, Zabbix needs to be aware of course, of what is available in our infrastructure and more importantly, what devices do we need to monitor. That's why the first step is to add devices to the Zabbix hosts list.

For each device that we monitor we also have to tell Zabbix what interfaces there are available on our host, what IP they use and on what port the communication passes.

This way our monitoring solution is aware of what we want to monitor and what the IP address, port, and so on is.

We will see later that when we add items, we can define in our item what interface to use from our host.

See also

► `https://www.zabbix.com/documentation/2.4/manual/config/hosts/host`

Creating host groups

So let's go a bit deeper into groups and see how to create them and link them with existing hosts. This duplicates the previous sentence. A host needs to be added to at least one group. Similar kind of hosts are grouped together even when the infrastructure is small.

Getting ready...

You should have a running Zabbix installation and you should have the knowledge of the definitions. To be able to add groups, you also need frontend access through an admin or super admin account.

How to do it...

1. From the Zabbix menu **Configuration** go to **Host groups**.

CONFIGURATION OF HOST GROUPS		
Host groups		
Displaying **1** to **6** of **6** found		
☐ **Name** ↑	**#**	**Members**
☐ Discovered hosts	Templates (0) Hosts (0)	-
☐ Hypervisors	Templates (0) Hosts (0)	-
☐ Linux servers	Templates (0) Hosts (0)	-
☐ Templates	Templates (38) Hosts (0)	Template OS Linux, Template App Zabbix Server, Template App Zabbix Proxy, Template App Zabbix Agent, Disks, Template SNMP OS Linux, Template SNMP Processors, Template IPMI Intel SR1530, Template IPMI Template OS Solaris, Template OS Mac OS X, Template OS Windows, Template JMX Generic, Template JM Template App HTTP Service, Template App HTTPS Service, Template App IMAP Service, Template App L Service, Template App SSH Service, Template App Telnet Service, Template ICMP Ping
☐ Virtual machines	Templates (0) Hosts (0)	-
☐ Zabbix servers	Templates (0) Hosts (1)	Zabbix server

| Enable selected ▼ | Go (0) |

Zabbix 2.4.3 Copyright 2001-2014 by Zabbix SIA

2. To add a new group, press the **Create host group** button and fill in a new name for the group in the **Group name** box.

3. When you want to move existing servers to the new group then select from **Other hosts | Group**, an existing host or group and move them to the column on the left with the arrow buttons. Those are the servers you want to add to your new host group.

4. Click the **Save** button at the bottom to save your changes.

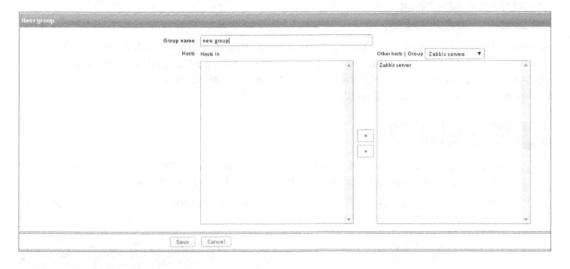

How it works...

When we first create a group, we have an overview of the groups already available on our system. When you start with a clean installation, there are already some groups available; most importantly, the group **Templates** where all templates are grouped together and **Zabbix servers** where your Zabbix server is added and where you can put other Zabbix servers. Host groups in Zabbix are a logical way of putting servers in a group that have the same specifications, for example, all Linux servers, Windows servers, and so on.

Zabbix will never overwrite the standard templates when you upgrade but it can be good practice to create a template group just for your own or modified templates.

See also

▶ https://www.zabbix.com/documentation/2.4/manual/config/hosts/host

Creating users

Sooner or later, you probably want to add extra users to Zabbix. You probably don't want them to have access to all servers and you probably don't want them to have all rights either. So it is now time to show you how to create new users in Zabbix.

Getting ready...

Just as with groups, we need a working Zabbix installation and a user with super admin permissions, A normal admin account will not do this time. The standard admin account automatically created when installing Zabbix is a super admin account. It can also be handy if you have some hosts already added to you setup.

How to do it...

1. To create a new user we go to the menu **Administration | Users** where we will get an overview of all existing user groups already available on the system.

2. Next we choose **Users** from the dropdown menu on the top right corner of the screen and click the **Create user** button.

| User | Media | Permissions |

Alias	
Name	
Surname	
Groups	[Add]
Password	
Password (once again)	
Language	English (en_GB) ▼
Theme	System default ▼
Auto-login	☐
Auto-logout (min 90 seconds)	☑ 900
Refresh (in seconds)	30
Rows per page	50
URL (after login)	

[Save] [Cancel]

3. In the **Alias** field, you will put the name that you want to use later when logging into Zabbix.

4. In the fields **Name**, **Surname** and **Password**, you obviously fill in the requested information.

5. In the **Groups** box, you add the groups where you want the user to belong to. Groups in Zabbix play an important role in the way that permissions will be placed on groups and not on users. So it's the rights on the group that will decide if the user will have access to certain servers or server groups or not.

6. The **Language** and **Theme** box speak for themselves and should not need more explanation.

7. The **Auto-login** box can be marked if you would like to log in automatically the next time you go to the Zabbix front page. Zabbix will make use of cookies and log you in automatically for the next 30 days.

8. **Auto-logout** is the opposite of auto-login, it will log you out of Zabbix automatically after *x* number of seconds of inactivity. The minimum is 90 seconds.

9. The **Refresh (in seconds)** option can be adjusted to your needs and will auto-refresh the data for graphs, screens, data, and so on. The refresh can be disabled by 0.

10. The **Rows per page** option can be altered to the number of rows that will be displayed in Zabbix in lists.

11. **URL (after login)** explains itself too. After logging in you will be transferred to the specified URL.

> The **URL (after login)** option is very useful for a user account that is being used in a helpdesk to automatically transfer the user to, for example, a screen or map.

12. The **Media** tab next to the **User** tab on top is where the user defines all the media that can be used for sending notifications. It is needed that the user or admin defines this or else the user will not be able to receive any messages.

13. When we click on **Add**, a popup window will appear where we can choose the **Type** of media we want to use and configure. This can be **Email**, **Jabber**, or **SMS**.

14. Next we select where we want our message to be sent to in the **Send to** box. Depending on the media type this will be an e-mail address, jabber account, or telephone number.

15. In the box **When active** we will feed in the time and the days of the week that this type of media will be active. This can be only during certain hours or certain days in the week.

16. **Use if severity** can be used to only get notifications from problems with a certain severity level. For example, we may choose that we only should get warnings from triggers with severity level **Disaster** by selecting only **Disaster**.

17. The **Status** box speaks for itself. This is just to disable or enable our chosen media.

18. This brings us to the last and probably the most important tab, **Permissions**. Zabbix will allow users access to certain parts of the menu based on the **User type**. Users will only be allowed to access certain servers depending on the rights their user group has on the host(s) or the host group that contains the host(s).

19. From the **User type** dropdown box, we can select three options. Depending on the user type we select, our user will have more or less access to the menus in Zabbix:

  ❏ **Zabbix User**: This user only has permissions to the **Monitoring** menu. The user has no access to any host groups by default. Permission to any host group must be explicitly assigned.

  ❏ **Zabbix Admin**: This user will have access to the **Monitoring** and **Configuration** menus. The user has no access to any host groups by default. Permissions to any host group must be explicitly assigned.

  ❏ **Zabbix Super Admin**: This user has the right to access everything in the **Configuration**, **Monitoring** and **Administration** menus. The user also has read/write access to all the hosts and host groups. Permissions cannot be revoked by denying access to host groups.

| User | Media | Permissions |

| User type | Zabbix User |

Host groups

Read-write	Read only	Deny
		Discovered hosts
		Hypervisors
		Linux servers
		Templates
		Virtual machines
		Zabbix servers

Hosts

		Template App FTP Service
		Template App HTTP Service
		Template App HTTPS Service
		Template App IMAP Service
		Template App LDAP Service
		Template App MySQL
		Template App NNTP Service
		Template App NTP Service
		Template App POP Service
		Template App SMTP Service
		Template App SSH Service
		Template App Telnet Service
		Template App Zabbix Agent
		Template App Zabbix Proxy
		Template App Zabbix Server

| Info | Permissions can be assigned for user groups only. |

| Save | Cancel |

Since Zabbix 2.2, write permissions will override read-only permissions. Before 2.2 this was not the case; so if you migrate from a previous version to 2.2 or higher, be careful to check the rights!

How it works...

As we have seen, depending on what kind of user we create, we will have more or less permissions to configure or administer Zabbix. Normal users and admins will start without any access permissions. Only the super admin user will start with all rights on all host groups and they can't be revoked. This means that permissions in Zabbix are set at the group-level and not at the user-level. However, alarms can only be set at the user-level.

See also...

  ▸ Have a look at the section in *Chapter 1, Frontend installation and configuration* where we have showed you how to configure alarms.

Creating user groups

As we have seen when creating users in Zabbix, we have to add users to groups. So let's have a look at how to create them and see why we need them.

Getting ready...

To be able to add user groups, we need a running Zabbix installation with an account that has super administration rights.

How to do it...

1. Go to **Administration | Users** and select from the dropdown on the right user groups. This will give you an overview of all user groups available in Zabbix.

2. Next click **Create user** group to create a new user group.

3. First field we can fill in is **Group name** this is obviously the name we want to give to our group.

4. The field **Users In group** is where we can add some users to our group. From the dropdown menu **Other groups**, we are able to show all users or some that already belong to another group.

5. The **Frontend access** selection box is how the users from that group will authenticate:

    ❏ **System default**: Use default authentication as set in the authentication menu.

    ❏ **Internal**: Use Zabbix authentication (ignored when using HTTP authentication)

- **Disabled**: GUI access is forbidden. The Enabled option is obviously to enable or disable our group. Debug mode will enable the debug mode for the users in our group.

6. When we switch from the **User group** tab to the **Permissions** tab, we are able to tell what access we will give to the users in our group.

7. Click on the **Add** button under **Read-write**, **Read only**, or **Deny** to add hosts or host groups to our user group to give the correct permissions:

- **Read only**: Members can read the values measured for those hosts and receive messages.

- **Read-write**: Members of this group can also configure those hosts.

- **Deny**: The user will not have access to these hosts. Even when permissions are granted in another group, they will still be refused.

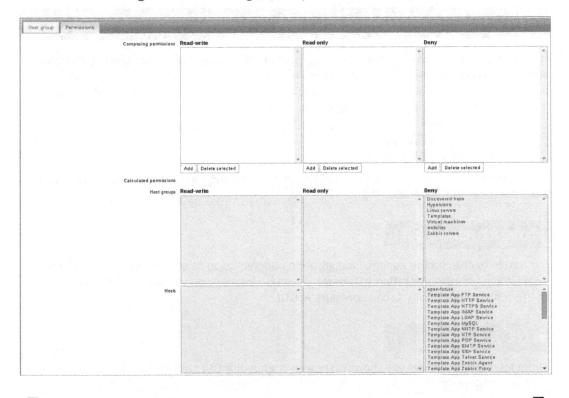

When giving read-write or write permissions to users, the user must also be admin to be able to view the **Configuration** tab. Else the user will not be able to edit the hosts. Also the admin user will not be able to link or unlink templates if he or she has no read access to the templates group.

How it works...

Users may belong to any number of user groups. Based on the group they belong to, the user will get access to certain servers. It is also possible that those groups have different access permissions to hosts. This means that a user can belong to a group with read-only permissions and write permissions to the same servers. In this case, the user will get read/write permissions. Since Zabbix 2.2, write permissions will take precedence over read-only permissions.

See also

▸ https://www.zabbix.com/documentation/2.4/manual/config/users_ and_usergroups/usergroup

General administration

Now that we have seen how to add users, groups, permissions, and more, there is still some administration possible in Zabbix that is more general. As super administrator, you have the right to configure the GUI, housekeeper, regular expressions, and more. We will show you in this topic what more there is to configure and how to do it.

Getting ready...

You probably know it already by now that you need a working Zabbix installation with a user that has super administration rights.

How to do it...

To be able to change the general configuration options, log in as super admin and go to the menu. Click on **Administration | General**, on your right side you will see a dropdown menu. The first parameter that you can configure is **GUI**.

GUI

In the following steps, we will show you how to change the GUI settings of your Zabbix configuration:

GUI

Default theme	Original blue ▼
Dropdown first entry	All ▼ ☑ remember selected
Search/Filter elements limit	1000
Max count of elements to show inside table cell	50
Enable event acknowledges	☑
Show events not older than (in days)	7
Max count of events per trigger to show	100
Show warning if Zabbix server is down	☑

Save

Let's have a look at the options:

1. The first option to change our GUI menu is **Default theme**. We have the option here to select the default theme for our Zabbix installation from the list of themes.

2. The **Dropdown first entry** option will let us choose when we select an element in a dropdown box, if it should display **None** or **All**. **Remember selected** box will remember our item selected and show this the next time we use the selection box.

3. The **Search/Filter elements limit** option is standard on 1000. This when changed, will limit the maximum number of rows that will be displayed in a web interface list, for example **Configuration | Hosts**.

4. The option **Max counts of elements to show inside a table cell**, on the other hand, will limit the entries that are displayed in a single table cell.

5. **Enable event acknowledges** option will let us chose if events can be acknowledged or not in the Zabbix interface.

6. While the option **Show events not older than (in days)** will limit the number of days for events displayed in the **Status of Triggers** screen. Default is **7**.

7. The option **Max count of events per trigger to show** will limit the number of events shown for each trigger in the **Status of Triggers** screen. Standard is **100**.

8. The last option **Show warning if Zabbix server is down**, will give us a warning on top of the browser if the Zabbix server is down or cannot be reached.

Housekeeping

In the next steps of our recipe, we will explain you how to fine-tune the housekeeper settings in Zabbix:

CONFIGURATION OF HOUSEKEEPING

Housekeeping

Events and alerts	Enable internal housekeeping	☑
	Trigger data storage period (in days)	365
	Internal data storage period (in days)	365
	Network discovery data storage period (in days)	365
	Auto-registration data storage period (in days)	365
IT services	Enable internal housekeeping	☑
	Data storage period (in days)	365
Audit	Enable internal housekeeping	☑
	Data storage period (in days)	365
User sessions	Enable internal housekeeping	☑
	Data storage period (in days)	365
History	Enable internal housekeeping	☑
	Override item history period	☐
	Data storage period (in days)	90
Trends	Enable internal housekeeping	☑
	Override item trend period	☐
	Data storage period (in days)	365

Save   Reset defaults

1. The first thing we see in housekeeping is **Events and alerts** option. Here we can enable or disable housekeeper for events and alerts. We can also change how long data is kept for triggers, internal data, network discovery, and auto-registration. Housekeeper will do it's cleanup using the days specified here. Even we have set different values for our triggers in Zabbix, we can override them globally here.

2. Same goes for **IT services**, **Audit**, **User sessions**, **History**, and **Trends**. Here, we can choose to make use of housekeeper or not and choose how long we want to keep our data.

3. For **History** and **Trends**, there is an extra option available: **Override item history period** and **Override item trend period**. When we select this box, values will be globally set. Remember that we can set them for every item individually; when this box is marked those values will be overridden.

4. The button **Reset defaults** speaks for itself, when we push this button all variables will be reset. This means that any changes made will be undone.

Images

In this part of our recipe, we will show you where we can add images such as backgrounds and icons in Zabbix:

1. On top right, we have a dropdown box with **Icon** and **Background**. The icon box holds all icons that can be used in Zabbix maps.

2. The **Background** type will show all backgrounds that can be used in Zabbix maps.

3. Just above the dropdown box we have a button **Create Image**. This button allows us to add new icons and backgrounds to Zabbix.

Icon mapping

Icon mapping is what we use in Zabbix in maps to automatically map certain servers with certain types of icons. We will explain you how icons can be mapped in our Zabbix setup:

1. First box is **Name**; here we can put a name that we want to give to our mappings.

2. Next we have our **Mappings** box where we see **Inventory** field, **Expression** and **Icon**. Here we can map an Inventory field with some icon in Zabbix based on a certain expression. For example, we could select OS in inventory field and for expression give Linux and use a server icon with a penguin. This way all Linux servers would get an icon with a penguin, so we would know easily in our Zabbix map that our servers were running on Linux.

Regular expressions

Regular expressions can be used in Zabbix on certain places. Example: In low-level discovery we can make use of a regular expression on our filter for our filesystem.

CONFIGURATION OF REGULAR EXPRESSIONS

Expressions	Test

Name	

Expressions

Expression	Expression type	Case sensitive
Add		

Save   Cancel

1. The first box is as usual, the **Name** for our regular expression. Later we use this name to refer to our regular expression. When making use of regular expressions we put the @ symbol in front of our expression name.

2. The **Expressions** box is where we create our regular expressions. By pressing the **Add** button we get a box where we can write our **regexp**.

3. When we have created our regular expression we can test it by going to the **Test** tab on top, next to **Expressions**. Here we can put a word in the **Test string** box and click **Test expressions** to see if our output is **True** or **False**.

Macros

Here we will define the system-wide macros. System-wide macros can be used in Zabbix by anyone and we call them with the macro name. Example: `{$SNMP_COMMUNITY}`.

1. In our first box **Macro**, we will add the macro that we want to use. This has to be a keyword between **{ }** and with a **$** sign in front.

2. In the **Value** box, we will give the value that we want to assign to our macro.

Value mapping

In Zabbix we can create value maps. Value maps are a way in Zabbix to create a more human-readable format for the data that we have collected. Example: when our **Uninterruptible Power Supplies** (**UPS**) returns the value 1, we can map this in Zabbix with **Battery OK**. This way we know when our UPS returns the value of 1 that our battery is OK.

1. When we click **Create value map**, first thing to do of course, is give a name to our value mapping.

2. In the field **Value**, we put the value that we want to map. Based on our example with the UPS this would be 1.

3. In the next field **Mapped to**, we will put the value that we want to see. In our case this will be **Battery OK**.

 Since Zabbix 2.2, it is possible to map floats and characters. Before 2.2, it was only possible to map numeric (unsigned) data to text.

Working time

When you see this box, you probably think that this option is to determine when Zabbix will be available to people and not. Nothing could be further from the truth. In this box, we put our working hours, but the time and days from this box will be used in our graphs. In our graphs, the working time will have a white background while the non-working hours will have a grey background.

1. In the box **Working time** we put the working time based on the following format:
   - **d-d,hh:mm-hh:mm** : where **d** is the day of the week, **h** stands for hours and **m** for minutes.
2. It is possible to put multiple periods together. This can be done by separating them with a semicolon **;**. For example: In the week from 9 till 17 h and in the weekend from 9 till 12:
   - 1-5,09:00-17:00;6-7,09:00-12:00

Trigger severities

Remember when we build triggers in Zabbix, we need to add a severity level to the trigger we have build to let us know how bad our issue is. The names can be changed in Zabbix but the amount of severity levels cannot be changed:

Trigger severities

	Custom severity	Colour	
Not classified	Not classified	DBDBDB	
Information	Information	D6F6FF	
Warning	Warning	FFF6A5	
Average	Average	FFB689	
High	High	FF9999	
Disaster	Disaster	FF3838	

Info	Custom severity names affect all locales and require manual translation!

Save   Reset defaults

1. In the box **Custom severity**, we can give a new name to each severity. However, custom severity names affect all locales and require manual translation!

2. In the box **Colour**, we can click on the color and choose a new color or we can put the HTML color code in the box, if you know this from your head.

3. The **Reset defaults** button will reset all changes made and revert back to the original settings.

Trigger displaying options

The colors for acknowledged and/or unacknowledged events can be customized and blinking can be enabled or disabled. Also, the time period for displaying OK triggers and for blinking upon trigger status change can be customized.

Other parameters

The **Other parameters** is a collection of other parameters in Zabbix that can be altered. Those settings don't really belong into a specific group, so they were brought together under the name **Other parameters**:

Other parameters	
Refresh unsupported items (in sec)	600
Group for discovered hosts	Discovered hosts ⬍
User group for database down message	Zabbix administrators ⬍
Log unmatched SNMP traps	☑

Save

1. Our first box **Refresh unsupported items (in sec)** will try to refresh our unsupported items in Zabbix every *x* number of seconds. When we put 0, automatic activation will be disabled.

2. The option **Group for discovered hosts** will place hosts discovered by network discovery and agent auto-registration automatically in the group selected here.

3. The option **User group for database down message** will inform the group selected here in case of a disaster when the database is down. When the database goes down Zabbix will start sending alarms until the issue is resolved.

4. The option **Log unmatched SNMP traps** when enabled, will log all SNMP traps if no corresponding interface was found.

How it works...

Under **Administration | General** we have a lot of settings in Zabbix that we need to check. Some of the settings are for the frontend but others are there to make sure Zabbix keeps working (housekeeper), while other settings are needed to make our life more easy and filter certain unwanted data (macro's and regexp). All these settings can only be set as a super admin user in Zabbix. It's important that you spend some time on these settings as you probably will have to work a lot with regexp, macros, maps, triggers, and so on once you set up Zabbix in production.

See also

► More detailed information can be found in the online Zabbix documentation at:

```
https://www.zabbix.com/documentation/2.4/manual/web_interface/
frontend_sections/administration/general
```

Authenticating users

Now that we have seen most of the configuration options of Zabbix, it probably makes sense to talk about what options we have to authenticate users. Zabbix supports three authentication methods. In this topic, we will show you what methods can be used and how to configure them.

Getting ready...

As usual, you need a working Zabbix configuration. To be able to configure the authentication methods, we need an account with super admin privileges.

How to do it...

When we want to set up the way users authenticate with Zabbix, we have some choices to make. When we go to **Administration | Authentication**, the user authentication method can be changed:

1. The easiest way of authenticating people and also the standard way, is authentication done by Zabbix. For this to work, we select **Internal** as default authentication method. Nothing else has to be done here. All users will authenticate with the user and password that we created in the user administration panel. If you can't recollect how to do this, then go back to the section in the beginning of *Chapter 3*, *Creating users*.

2. Another more advanced way of authenticating people is by making use of **Lightweight Directory Access Protocol** (**LDAP**). When making use of this external authentication method, the users must exist in Zabbix as well but the password will be read from the LDAP instead from Zabbix.

3. Another possibility is to make use of the HTTP authentication method. For this to work, we select HTTP and that's it. This means, all users will be authenticated against a web server authentication mechanism.

In the case you would like to talk to an LDAP/**Active Directory** (**AD**) backend, we select the tab LDAP. In this part of the recipe, I will show you how to configure Zabbix to authenticate to an LDAP/AD backend:

1. First thing to do when selecting LDAP authentication is of course, telling Zabbix the IP address of the LDAP server. This information we put in the field **LDAP host**. For secure LDAP, make use of the LDAPS protocol. Example: `ldaps://`.

2. The **Port** number should normally be port `389` or `636` for secure LDAP. When connecting to AD on Windows 2008 R2 or later, try `3268` if a connection to `389` is not working.

3. **Base DN** is where you fill in the place where your users are in the LDAP or AD. `ou=Users`, `ou=system` for OpenLDAP.

4. The **Search attribute**, here you must use the sAMAccountName for AD or the UID for OpenLDAP.

5. In **Bind DN**, you will have to fill in an existing user. The users must have a non-expiring password and no special rights on the AD/LDAP. This account is for binding and searching in the LDAP server.

6. **Bind password** speaks for itself here. You have to add the password for the LDAP user.

7. **Test authentication** is just a header for the testing section.

8. **Login** is where you have to put a name for test users. The users must exist in the LDAP and must also exist in Zabbix. Zabbix will not activate LDAP authentication if it cannot authenticate this user.

9. **User password** is of course, the password for our test user.

When you authenticate users from AD or LDAP it is always a good idea to create a new group, for example, internal users, and set its GUI access to **Internal** instead of system default. This way if you add the admin user to this group, you will always have access to the Zabbix server even when the AD or LDAP is unreachable.

How it works...

When selecting **Internal**, all information comes from Zabbix. Users and passwords will come from Zabbix. When selecting **HTTP**, we need to have an external authentication system in place on our web server. There are a plenty of authentication mechanisms on Apache and all of them should work.

When using LDAP, we need to have an LDAP or AD authentication system in place with all our users in it already. Users should also exist in Zabbix but their passwords will be read from the LDAP. Same rules apply for HTTP.

4

Monitoring with Zabbix

In this chapter, we will cover the following topics:

- Active agents
- Passive agents
- Extending agents
- Simple checks
- SNMP checks
- Internal checks
- Zabbix trapper
- IPMI checks
- JMX checks
- Aggregate checks
- External checks
- Database monitoring
- Checks with SSH
- Checks with Telnet
- Calculated checks
- Building web scenarios
- Monitoring web scenarios
- Some advanced monitoring tricks
- Autoinventory

Introduction

Now that we know how to set up a Zabbix server and configure it, we will see what is the difference between active and a passive agent configuration. After we know the difference between the agent setups, we will see all the different kinds of ways to do checks which helps monitoring other servers with Zabbix. Those checks will help you in setting up different ways to monitor your devices.

Active agents

Hope you recollect what we discussed in *Chapter 1, Agent installation and configuration*. We talked about active and passive agent configurations. In this topic, we will explain a bit more in depth the active agent setup in Zabbix. Remember when we create items in Zabbix, we can create Zabbix items as passive and active.

Getting ready

You will need a Zabbix server and you must have the software for the agent installed on the machine that you would like to monitor. This can be the Zabbix server or another machine. The agent needs no configuration. We will explain you how to go about the same in this recipe.

How to do it ...

1. The first thing we do is make sure that our agent has the proper configuration setup to work as an active agent. Make sure that in the `zabbix_agentd.conf` file the `ServerActive` option is set and points to the Zabbix server.

2. Make sure that our server can be reached on port 10051. Verify that the port is open in the firewall!

3. Next in the agent configuration file we need to set the hostname; this name must be unique and must be set exactly the same as in host configuration on the server. This can be found under **Configuration | Hosts**.

4. Restart the `zabbix_agent` option (`service zabbix-agent restart` for Red Hat 7 users this is `systemctl restart zabbix-agent.service`).

5. Check the agent log in tail `-f /var/log/zabbix/zabbix_agentd.log` for errors.

6. You are now ready to add an active item on your host. Go to **Configuration | Hosts | Items | Create item**.

Item	
Name	
Type	Zabbix agent (active) ⇕
Key	⬚ Select

How it works

The active agent will initiate the communication with the Zabbix server and pull out a list of items it has to check from the server.

The agent knows from the `ServerActive` parameter in the `zabbix_agentd.conf` file, what servers it has to contact. The option `RefreshActiveChecks` is the parameter that will control how many times the agent has to ask for this list. The standard value is 120 seconds. This means, that if we change something in our Zabbix configuration in an active item, it can take up to 2 minutes before our active agent will be aware of the change and 1 minute extra for the Zabbix server to refresh its cache. (`CacheUpdateFrequency`)

The active agent also has the advantage of having a buffer. The standard value that data is kept is 5 seconds but can be increased up to 1 hour with the `BufferSend` parameter.

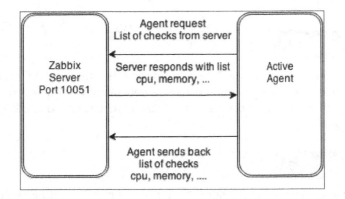

There's more

When we make use of the active agent, it is possible to send our checks to more than only one server or proxy. We can do this by adding a list of comma-separated IP addresses to the option `ServerActive` in our agent `config` file.

If you configure the agent as an active agent, then it's best to not fill in the `Server` option in the agent configuration file as this is for the passive agent. (Be careful with this, as `Server` and `ServerActive` are two different options in the configuration file).

See also

> ▶ If you would like to know more about protocols being used, how communication between agent and server is set up and so on then you could look into the Zabbix documentation.
>
> ```
> https://www.zabbix.com/documentation/2.4/manual/appendix/items/
> activepassive
> ```

Passive agents

In this topic, we will show you how to setup your agent as a passive agent only. We will see how to create a passive item for our agent and have a look at how the communication works with our Zabbix server.

Getting ready

For this recipe to work, you need your Zabbix server and the standard login account admin or another super administration account. We also need a host with the agent installed. This can be on another host or on our Zabbix server. There is no need to configure the host configuration file yet.

How to do it ...

1. The first thing we do is make sure that our agent has the proper configuration setup to work as a passive agent. Make sure that in the `zabbix_agentd.conf` file the `ServerActive` option is not set and that the option `Server` is set and points to the Zabbix server.

2. Remember that the hostname is only for the active agent, so we don't need to define this parameter.

3. Restart the **Zabbix agent** (`service zabbix-agent restart` or RHEL 7 users run `systemctl restart zabbix-agent.service`).

4. You are now ready to add a passive item on your host, go to **Configuration | Hosts | Items | Create item**.

Item	
Name	
Type	Zabbix agent
Key	Select

 See how **Type** is just **Zabbix agent** and not **Zabbix agent (passive)** like we had for the active checks.

How it works

Passive checks are really simple in the way that the server or proxy will ask the agent for some data such as CPU load, disk space, and so on. The Zabbix agent will then give the requested data back to the Zabbix server or proxy:

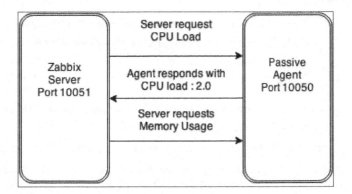

There's more...

Same as with the active agent, we can add more than one IP address as server or proxy in our passive agent's configuration file. To do this we also add a list of comma-separated IP addresses or hostnames.

 As you can see, there is more communication between the passive agent and the server than with the active agent and the server. This means that more sockets will be opened on the server side. So in a large setup, you could possibly run out of sockets if you have a lot of passive agents running without a proxy. Also, the passive agent has no buffer such as the active agent.

Extending agents

Now that you know how to install and configure a Zabbix agent, let's go a bit deeper into the monitoring aspect of the agent. A monitoring system would quickly reach its limits if we don't expand it with our own checks. Many companies require specific checks that are not available as item on our agent. There are a few ways to extend Zabbix, one solution is to work with user parameters. We will see how to extend our agent to monitor beyond the limits of Zabbix.

Getting ready

We need a Zabbix server and a Zabbix agent properly configured. The easiest way is probably by making use of the Zabbix agent that is installed on your Zabbix server.

How to do it ...

1. First thing we can do is extend our agent with user parameters. This must be done in the `zabbix_agentd.conf` file.

2. Extend the agent with the `UserParameter` option such as in this example:

    ```
    UserParameter=mysql.threads,mysqladmin -u root -p<password>
    status|cut -f3 -d":"|cut -f1 -d"Q"
    ```

3. This will return the number of MySQL threads to item `mysql.threads` (-p is only needed if you have configured a MySQL `root` password).

4. Restart the Zabbix agent after you have saved the configuration file.

5. In our Zabbix server create a new item on the host where we have added the `UserParameter` option.

6. Add a new **Name**, example `Mysql threads`.

7. Select **Type**; this can be `Zabbix agent` or `Zabbix agent (active)`.

8. Create a new item **Key** named `mysql.threads`.

9. Select as **Type of information** `Numeric (unsigned)`.

10. For **Data type** we select `Decimal`.

11. All other settings can be left as is.

12. Go to latest data page **Monitoring | Latest data** and after some time, your item `Mysql Threads` will be populated with a number.

Item	
Name	Mysql Threads
Type	Zabbix agent (active) ↕
Key	mysql.threads Select
Type of information	Numeric (unsigned) ↕
Data type	Decimal ↕

How it works

The `UserParameter` option that we put in the agent `config` file has the following syntax:

```
UserParameter=<key>,<command>
```

As you can see is the first option, a key; the key is necessary when configuring an item. You can enter a key here of your own choice, but the key must be unique for each host.

Later when we configure our item in Zabbix, we make use of the same key for our item **Key**. We can make use of points and or underscores but no spaces or other special characters.

Behind our key we put a , followed with a command. This command is the command that's going to be executed by the Zabbix agent. In this example, we used a MySQL command. Of course, Zabbix is not limited to MySQL alone. We could check for example, some parameters from our OS.

There's more...

You can also pass options to the `UserParameter` via the Zabbix server.

```
UserParameter = some.key[*],somescript.sh $1 $2
```

The `[*]` in our key will make it possible for us to determine an unlimited number of items starting with `some.key` parameter when we create our item in the Zabbix server:

```
some.key[1] , some.key[2]
```

The value in our **Key** will then be passed in our script as `$1`, `$2`, and so on.

To make things more understandable, let's have a look at how we can improve our example `mysql.threads`.

```
UserParameter=mysql.threads[*],mysqladmin -u$1 -p$2 status|cut -f3
-d":"|cut -f1 -d"Q"
```

If we now add in Zabbix a item with key `mysql.threads[root,password]` then `$1` will be `root` and `$2` will be our password.

Remember that the Zabbix agent will run all `UserParameter` as the user you configured Zabbix to run as. Normally this will be the user `zabbix`. Sometimes the command you want to execute needs `root` privileges. To ensure that the Zabbix agent is allowed to execute such programs you can make use of the `sudo` command. Add the appropriate program in the `/etc/sudoers` file with `visudo`.

```
Zabbix ALL = (ALL) NOPASSWD: /usr/bin/someprogram
```

Also, make sure that you comment the rule `Defaults requiretty`. Else you will get error messages in the log file telling you that you are required to have a `tty`.

See also

▸   https://www.zabbix.com/documentation/2.4/manual/config/items/
    userparameters

Simple checks

In this topic, we will explain you the use of simple checks in Zabbix. Simple checks are checks that can be run from the Zabbix server without the need of a Zabbix agent on the host.

Getting ready

For simple checks, we need a Zabbix server properly configured with super administrator rights. We don't need a Zabbix agent for this setup. What we do need is a host where we can test our simple check. This can be any device as long as it is reachable on the network by our Zabbix server.

How to do it ...

1. On the Zabbix host that we want to check we create a new item. Go to **Configuration | Hosts | Item | Create item** (Remember normally in production we create items in templates but for our test a local item if just fine).

2. First thing to do in our item is put a visible **Name** for our item.

3. The we select the item **Type**. In our case this will be `Simple check`.

4. Next thing we do is replace the options in our **Key** in my case I removed the first option target so the **Host Interface** selected will be used. If you don't want to use the options then you can just put the **,** and not fill in the option such as `<target>`, `<packet>` and so on.

5. `<target>` : Host IP address or DNS name.

6. `<packets>` : Number of packets (default is 3, min is 1).

7. `<interval>` : Time between successive packets in milliseconds (default is 1000 ms, min is 20 ms).

8. `<size>` : packet size in bytes (default is 56 bytes on x86, 68 bytes on x86_64, min is 24 bytes).

9. `<timeout>` : timeout in ms (default is 500 ms, min is 50 ms).

10. Then with the **Select** button we select a **Key** for our item from the list of standard available keys. In this example I will make use of the `icmpping` item.

11. **User name** and **Password** are only used in simple checks for VMware monitoring.

12. Next we select the **Type of information**. This will be `Numeric (unsigned)` as we have selected `icmpping` as key we will only get a value back of 0 or 1.

13. **Data type** in our case will be `Decimal`.

14. All other values should be fine as they are:

Item	
Name	Ping Check
Type	Simple check
Key	icmpping[,20,50,256,100] — Select
Host interface	127.0.0.1 : 10050
User name	
Password	
Type of information	Numeric (unsigned)
Data type	Decimal

How it works

Zabbix simple checks, checks by ICMP ping or by port scan if a host is online and whether the service accepts connections. There is no need for a Zabbix agent to use this method of checking. The Zabbix server is 100 percent responsible for the complete process. The return values of the simple checks are either 1 or 0 (numerically unsigned) when we check the availability of a host or port. When we do performance checks the value returned will be measured in seconds (numeric (float)). When this check fails, a value of 0 will be returned.

There's more...

Zabbix relies on **fping** and **fping6** for the `icmppingsec`, `icmpping` and `icmppingloss` checks. Make sure that fping6 is available and the proper SUID permissions are set.

```
# which fping (this command will there us where the location of fping is)
/sbin/fping
# ll /sbin/fping
-rwsr-xr-x. 1 root root 32960 Oct 26 11:40 /sbin/fping
```

(Make sure that permissions for user are set to `rws` as in this example).

As fping is a third party tool Zabbix relies on, there can be some issue. Depending on your distribution, another version of fping with different options can be installed. With fping3, this issue should be resolved. Users of RHEL 6.x and 7.x or derivatives can be sure that the correct version comes with their distribution.

 It's possible to use Zabbix with ping instead of fping, however fping is more efficient and can ping several hosts simultaneously. So it's better to stay with fping. If fping always returns 0 as value to Zabbix, please check SELinux. (`https://www.zabbix.com/forum/showthread.php?t=40523`).

See also

Zabbix supports more than just the `icmpping` item. For a full list with all options in detail, take a look at the Zabbix documentation.

If you make use of IPv6 then you need to have fping6 installed on your system.

`https://www.zabbix.com/documentation/2.4/manual/config/items/itemtypes/simple_checks`.

SNMP checks

What would monitoring be like if there was no support for the SNMP? SNMP is a well-known and widely used standard in lots of devices. Therefore, we will see in this topic, how to configure our Zabbix server to be able to retrieve data provided by SNMP.

Getting ready

Make sure that you have setup your Zabbix server properly. For this recipe we also need a host configured in our Zabbix server that supports SNMP (don't forget to add the `snmp` interface). If you have compiled your server from source (this you should only do for non-production systems), then don't forget to compile it with the option `-with-net-snmp`. To be able to make use of the SNMP tools, we need to make sure the `net-snmp-utils` package is installed.

How to do it ...

1. First thing to do is add a new **Host** in our Zabbix server and fill in all settings for the **SNMP interfaces**.

2. Install the `net-snmp-utils` package.

   ```
   # yum install net-snmp-utils
   ```

3. Then create a new **Item** on our host or better still, add a new **Item** to a template.

4. Next we find out the **Object Identifier** (**OID**) of the item that we want to monitor from our device. This can be done with a tool such as: **snmpwalk**.

   ```
   snmpwalk -v 2c -c public 192.168.10.1 | more
   ```

5. Where **2c** is the supported version and **public** is the community string. Zabbix supports SNMP v1, 2c and 3.

6. Now if all goes well when we used the correct version and community string, we should get a lot of information back from snmpwalk. If we wanted to monitor the number of `inOctets` on port 1 we would filter out this line:

   ```
   IF-MIB::ifInOctets.1 = Counter32: 1362407
   ```

7. Now that we have found the correct OID for our item, we can also look for the numeric OID if we want. This can be done with a tool called : **snmpget**.

   ```
   snmpget -v 2c -c public 192.168.10.1 -On IF-MIB::ifInOctets.1
   ```

8. We would get back from our device some output like the following line:

   ```
   .1.3.6.1.2.1.2.2.1.10.1 = Counter32: 1494804
   ```

9. If we want to make use of the full OID, then we can look this up with the following command:

   ```
   snmpget -v 2c -c public 192.168.10.1 -Of IF-MIB::ifInOctets.1
   ```

10. Our output would then look like this:

```
.iso.org.dod.internet.mgmt.mib-2.interfaces.ifTable.ifEntry.
ifInOctets.1 = Counter32: 1566936
```

11. Now finally we have enough data to create our **Item**, so fill in the item details where you select for **Type** the correct SNMP version. Both short, long or numeric OID's can be used in Zabbix.

12. **Key** can be anything you like that makes sense.

13. **Host Interface** has to be the correct SNMP interface from our host.

14. In **SNMP OID** we put the correct OID that we got back from `snmpget`.

15. Next we fill in the **SNMP community**. This is our community string.

16. **Port** is the port on our host to communicate with. This should standardly be `161`.

17. **Type of information** in our case is `Numeric (float)`.

18. **Units** is where we fill in **Bytes** as Zabbix monitors in bytes.

19. **Store value** should be `Delta(speed per seconds)` this will calculate the delta speed per second and is what we need for our network data.

20. The other parameters such as custom multiplier, store value and so on depends on the kind of data you want to monitor.

Another way to do some SNMP monitoring is to make use of dynamic indexes in Zabbix. Sometimes this makes sense as the OID number won't stay the same. Index numbers may be dynamic, they may change over time after an update and then our monitoring solution will stop working.

1. Let's go back to our network card and do a `snmpwalk` to find out the OID that we need to use for the network card on our **Network Attached Storage (NAS)**:

```
# snmpwalk -v 2c -c public 192.168.10.1 | grep ifDesc
IF-MIB::ifDescr.1 = STRING: eth0
IF-MIB::ifDescr.2 = STRING: lo
```

2. From the `ifDescr.1` parameter, we know that our index is `1`. So we know that the `ifOutOctets` for eth0 is this line:

```
# snmpwalk -v 2c -c public 192.168.10.1 | grep ifOutOctets.1
IF-MIB::ifOutOctets.1 = Counter32: 23843596
```

3. Dynamic indexing will take into consideration the possibility of an index number changing. For this, we make use of a special syntax in our SNMP OID. Let's see how to build our dynamic index with Zabbix from the data we have gathered:

Name	ifOutOctets $1
Type	SNMPv2 agent ▼
Key	ifOutOctets[Port1] Select
Host interface	192.168.10.1 : 161 ▼
SNMP OID	IF-MIB::ifOutOctets["index","ifDescr","eth0"]
SNMP community	public
Port	161
Type of information	Numeric (float) ▼
Units	Bytes
Use custom multiplier	☐ 1
Update interval (in sec)	30
Flexible intervals	Interval Period Action
	No flexible intervals defined.
New flexible interval	Interval (in sec) 50 Period 1-7,00:00-24:00 Add
History storage period (in days)	90
Trend storage period (in days)	365
Store value	Delta (speed per second) ▼
Show value	As is ▼ show value mappings
New application	

4. When you look now at **Monitoring | Latest data**, you should get some new data for the item you have created.

How it works

First of all your device needs to support SNMP. An easy way is to check for connectivity with:

```
# snmpstatus -v 2c -c public <host IP>
```

This gives us back some basic information from the device we want to monitor:

```
# snmpstatus -v 2c -c public 192.168.10.1
[UDP: [192.168.10.1]:161->[0.0.0.0]]=>[Linux NAS 2.6.15 #1636 Sun Oct 23
04:20:59 CST 2011 armv5tejl] Up: 0:05:16.95
Interfaces: 2, Recv/Trans packets: 2908/3112 | IP: 2947/3074
```

If all goes well, we get some data back that tells us that we made a connection on port `161` and that we made use of the **User Datagram Protocol** (**UDP**) protocol and that our device is a NAS. If this is not working, check with the `-v 1` command to make sure the device supports version 2c and also verify on your device if the community string is set to public.

Zabbix supports protocols v1, v2c, and v3. When you read out the information from your device with snmpwalk, you need to specify:

```
# snmpwalk -v <version> -c <community string> <host IP>
```

This will generate a lot of data so best is to put a **more** at the end to make it easier to scroll.

From this data you need to find out the numeric OID. This can be done with a tool called **snmpget**.

```
# snmpget -v <verion> -c <community string> -On <Host IP> <Data Base
OID>
```

The OID that we get here can be used in Zabbix in our item as SNMP OID.

How to know what OID to use? Not so easy to answer. You either know it or you have to ask the manufacturer or find it out with Google. There is no other easy way to get it.

When we want to make use of dynamic indexes in Zabbix, it gets a bit more complicated. Here we have to retrieve two SNMP values. This means that it can create a bit more overload on our server.

First, we will retrieve with `snmpwalk` the description (`ifDescr.1`) to find out what the index is; for our item in our example with eth0 the `index` was `1`. Then we can go and look for the actual desired information; in our case this was the `ifOutOctets.1`.

Now when we want to combine those two SNMP values into one, we have to do it like this:

Database OID	index,	ifDescr,	eth0

Let's have a look at these in further detail:

- ▶ **The database OID**: This is the base part of the OID that is keeping the data that we want to retrieve without the actual index

- ▶ **String index**: This cannot be changed and will always be index as currently only 1 method is supported

- ▶ **Index base OID**: The part of the OID that will be looked up so that we get the index value that corresponds to the string'

- ▶ **Index string**: This is our exact string that will be searched for

There's more...

If you don't have a SNMP device to do some testing it is possible to setup SNMP on your computer by:

1. Installing the `net-snmp` package.
2. Starting the `snmpd` service (`service snmpd start`).
3. The command `snmpwalk -v 2c -c public 127.0.0.1` should give you some output to work with.

Since Zabbix 2.2.3, Zabbix server and proxy query SNMP devices for multiple values in a single request (128 max). This makes monitoring SNMP devices more performant.

In Zabbix 2.4, there is an option in the `snmp` interface of the host to add bulk requests.

When monitoring devices with SNMP v3, it's important to check that the `snmpEngineID` parameter is never shared by two or more devices. Each device must have a unique ID else you would see a lot of errors in your `zabbix_server.log` file about the device being unreachable.

With some switches it is possible to force that the OID never changes, this can resolve the more complex setup of dynamic indexes.

To make use of SNMP v3 on your computer you can run the following commands:

```
# service snmpd stop
# net-snmp-create-v3-user -ro zabbix
Enter authentication pass-phrase:
adminadmin
Enter encryption pass-phrase:
  [press return to reuse the authentication pass-phrase]


adding the following line to /var/lib/net-snmp/snmpd.conf:
   createUser zabbix MD5 "adminadmin" DES
adding the following line to /etc/snmp/snmpd.conf:
   rouser zabbix
# service snmpd start
# vi ~/.snmp/snmp.conf
defVersion 3
defSecurityLevel authPriv
defSecurityName zabbix
defPassphrase adminadmin
# snmpwalk -v3 localhost system
```

Sometimes OIDs have only a numeric description and then it's quite difficult to find what the exact purpose of the OID is. Some vendors have **Management Information Base** (**MIB**) available for download that can be used to make the information more readable. Another place to find MIB's for your devices can be on some websites where the community collects them.

After you have downloaded your MIB file you have to copy the file to the correct location. This can be in `~.snmp/mibs` per user or global in the `/usr/share/snmp/mibs` file.

Next, open the MIB file and look for the first line with, in my case, the name:

```
SYNOLOGY-SYSTEM-MIB DEFINITIONS ::= BEGIN
```

We need the name before the word `DEFINITIONS`.

Next time we run `snmp`, we will hopefully get a more descriptive output:

```
snmpwalk -m +SYNOLOGY-SYSTEM-MIB -v 2c -c public 192.168.10.1
```

A more definitive solution is to add the MIB file to your `snmpd.conf` file. This can be done by editing `/etc/snmp/snmpd.conf` and adding to the file:

```
mibs +SYNOLOGY-SYSTEM-MIB
```

In case you are looking to configure SNMP traps, then I suggest you look at the zabbxi.org web page as SNMP Traps in Zabbix have to be configured mostly on OS level.

`http://zabbix.org/wiki/Start_with_SNMP_traps_in_Zabbix.`
`https://www.zabbix.com/documentation/2.4/manual/`
`config/items/itemtypes/snmptrap?s[]=snmp&s[]=traps.`
The rest of the configuration is done as *Zabbix trapper* item. You might want to read the recipe about Zabbix trapper in this chapter to understand how to use it. If you look for a MIB browser under Linux then you can make use of `tkmib`- a GUI that is provided by the `net-snmp-gui` package.

See also

▸ `https://www.zabbix.com/documentation/2.4/manual/config/items/itemtypes/snmp`

▸ `https://www.zabbix.com/documentation/2.4/manual/config/items/itemtypes/snmp/dynamicindex`

▸ `https://access.redhat.com/documentation/en-US/Red_Hat_Enterprise_Linux/6/html/Deployment_Guide/sect-System_Monitoring_Tools-Net-SNMP-Configuring.html`

Internal checks

We have already seen that Zabbix is great at monitoring hosts but Zabbix is not limited to just collecting information from other hosts. The Zabbix internal items are items Zabbix can monitor to give us some insights on what's going on under the hood. Monitoring the internals is probably not your first task when you start your setup. Zabbix is configured from the start to work well but when your installation grows you will see the need to tweak/optimize some settings.

Getting ready

What do we need for this topic? You need to have your Zabbix server up and running. Internal items are internal checks, so we don't need an agent. Zabbix is perfectly capable to monitor its internals without the help of an agent. You only need to make sure that you have super administration rights.

How to do it ...

1. On your host or in a template, go to items and click **Create item** to add a new item.

2. In the **Name** field add a name for the item.

3. For **Type**, we select `Zabbix internal`.

4. For the **Key**, we select `zabbix[process,<type>,<num>,<state>]`. Here we change the parameters as follows: `zabbix[process,poller,avg,busy]`.

5. The **Type of information** that Zabbix will send us back is `Numeric (float)`.

6. For **Units** we can add the `%`.

7. All other parameters can remain standard.

Item	
Name	Zabbix $4 $2 processes, in %
Type	Zabbix internal ▼
Key	zabbix[process,poller,avg,busy]　　　Select
Type of information	Numeric (float) ▼
Units	%
Use custom multiplier	☐ 　　　　1
Update interval (in sec)	60

How it works

Our Zabbix internal key consists of some options that we can and cannot change. In the case of our item process options cannot be changed. Process means we will time a process; in our case the **poller** process, so we replaced `type` with `poller`. We will monitor the average for all the poller processes that are in a busy state. To accomplish, this we had to replace `<num>` with `<avg>` to calculate the average data and `<state>` with `<busy>` to tell Zabbix to do this for all processes in a busy state.

Zabbix has provided templates for the Zabbix server and proxy to monitor internal items. These templates are called App Zabbix Server and App Zabbix Proxy. It's best to link these templates and monitor their data in the **Latest data** page from Zabbix.

Since Zabbix 2.4, internal checks are always processed by server or proxy regardless of the host maintenance status.

Internal checks are always calculated by Zabbix server or by Zabbix proxy if the host is monitored by a proxy.

There's more

Zabbix runs as a list of processes in the background. Each process that runs is responsible for some task. If you run the `ps` command as shown here, you will see multiple `zabbix_server` processes running. When you look closer, you will see that some of them are for pollers or trappers. Even with the identical process names, they all process different internal items:

```
[root@zabbix patrik]# ps -ef | grep zabbix_server
zabbix    2271       1  0 Jan02 ?        00:00:00 /usr/sbin/zabbix_server -c /etc/zabbix/zabbix_server.conf
zabbix    2653    2271  0 Jan02 ?        00:18:53 /usr/sbin/zabbix_server: configuration syncer [synced configuration in 0.
138518 sec, idle 60 sec]
zabbix    2654    2271  0 Jan02 ?        00:01:16 /usr/sbin/zabbix_server: db watchdog [synced alerts config in 0.022220 se
c, idle 60 sec]
zabbix    2655    2271  0 Jan02 ?        00:18:31 /usr/sbin/zabbix_server: poller #1 [got 0 values in 0.000007 sec, idle 1
sec]
zabbix    2657    2271  0 Jan02 ?        00:18:22 /usr/sbin/zabbix_server: poller #2 [got 0 values in 0.000007 sec, idle 1
sec]
zabbix    2658    2271  0 Jan02 ?        00:18:29 /usr/sbin/zabbix_server: poller #3 [got 0 values in 0.000007 sec, idle 1
sec]
zabbix    2659    2271  0 Jan02 ?        00:18:27 /usr/sbin/zabbix_server: poller #4 [got 6 values in 0.010284 sec, idle 1
sec]
zabbix    2660    2271  0 Jan02 ?        00:18:28 /usr/sbin/zabbix_server: poller #5 [got 2 values in 0.096888 sec, idle 1
sec]
zabbix    2661    2271  0 Jan02 ?        00:00:51 /usr/sbin/zabbix_server: unreachable poller #1 [got 0 values in 0.000010
sec, idle 5 sec]
zabbix    2662    2271  0 Jan02 ?        00:04:06 /usr/sbin/zabbix_server: trapper #1 [processed data in 0.000975 sec, wait
ing for connection]
zabbix    2663    2271  0 Jan02 ?        00:04:09 /usr/sbin/zabbix_server: trapper #2 [processed data in 0.003770 sec, wait
ing for connection]
zabbix    2664    2271  0 Jan02 ?        00:04:09 /usr/sbin/zabbix_server: trapper #3 [processed data in 0.000870 sec, wait
ing for connection]
zabbix    2667    2271  0 Jan02 ?        00:04:13 /usr/sbin/zabbix_server: trapper #4 [processed data in 0.000865 sec, wait
ing for connection]
zabbix    2669    2271  0 Jan02 ?        00:04:13 /usr/sbin/zabbix_server: trapper #5 [processed data in 0.000424 sec, wait
ing for connection]
zabbix    2670    2271  0 Jan02 ?        00:09:56 /usr/sbin/zabbix_server: icmp pinger #1 [got 0 values in 0.000027 sec, id
le 5 sec]
zabbix    2671    2271  0 Jan02 ?        00:00:43 /usr/sbin/zabbix_server: alerter [sent alerts: 0 success, 0 fail in 0.001
292 sec, idle 30 sec]
```

When we want to monitor our Zabbix internal processes, it's good to know that they are split up and have different responsibilities.

- **Alerter**: This is the process responsible for sending messages.
- **Configuration syncer**: This is responsible for loading configuration data from the database into the cache.
- **DB watchdog**: This will check if our database is available and log this when it is not the case.
- **Discoverer**: This process will scan the network (autodiscovery).
- **Escalator**: This is process the escalations.
- **History syncer**: This process writes data collected into the database.
- **HTTP poller**: This is the process needed for Website Monitoring (scenarios).
- **Housekeeper**: This process that deletes old data from the database.
- **ICMP pinger**: This process is responsible for the ping of hosts.

- **IPMI poller**: This process will collect data via IPMI.

- **Node watcher**: The process is responsible for data exchange in a distributed monitoring (deprecated since 2.4).

- **Self-monitoring**: The process is responsible for the collection of internal data.

- **Poller**: The process responsible for the collection of data from Zabbix Agent (passive) and SNMP.

- **Proxy poller**: The process is responsible for collecting data from passive proxies.

- **Timer**: This process will execute the time-dependent triggers (nodata ()).

- **Trapper**: This process will accept all incoming data of active agents, Zabbix sender and active proxies.

- **Unreachable**: This service will contact unreachable hosts to see if they might be available again.

We can increase these values in the `zabbix_server.conf` file. After we change them keep in mind that you have to restart the server. Also, more processes mean that the Zabbix server will require more resources; so don't go to crazy on them but also don't be too sparse, for example, a shortage in pollers can result in items becoming unavailable for some time.

See also

- This is only one example and there are plenty more internal items that we can monitor with Zabbix. Take a look on the Zabbix website for a full list.

  `https://www.zabbix.com/documentation/2.4/manual/config/items/itemtypes/internal`

Zabbix trapper

Zabbix supports many ways to monitor our devices but sometimes we just want that little extra that is not possible out of the box with all the tools provided such as agents, IPMI, SNMP, and so on. But even when it seems impossible to monitor, Zabbix has a solution ready. Zabbix provides **zabbix_sender**, a tool to send data that we have gathered by, for example, our own scripts. This data will then be sent to the Zabbix server. The data sent to the server will be gathered by the Zabbix trapper.

Getting ready

To be able to finish this task successfully, we need a Zabbix server and a host with the zabbix_sender tool installed on our host.

How to do it...

► Make sure you have the zabbix_sender tool installed on a host in your network. This can be done from the Zabbix repositories by running the following command:

```
yum install zabbix-sender -y
```

► Next step is to create an item on our host. **Configuration | Hosts | Items | Create item**.

► Fill in the **Name** of your item.

► Select Zabbix trapper as **Type**.

► Insert some unique **Key** that you want to use (example: trapper.key).

► Select the correct **Type of information** and **Data type** of the value that you will return to the Zabbix server (in our case that is a numeric decimal).

► Now run zabbix_sender -z <ip-zabbixserver> -s <hostname agent> -k <item_key> -o <value>.

► In our case, this will look like: the zabbix_sender -z 192.168.10.102 -s "some host" -k trapper.key -o 20 command.

► Now when you go to **Monitoring | Latest data**, you will see the value you have sent to the Zabbix server. In our case 20.

Item		
Name	Zabbix Sender	
Type	Zabbix trapper ▼	
Key	trapper.key	Select
Type of information	Numeric (unsigned) ▼	
Data type	Decimal ▼	
Units		
Use custom multiplier	☐ 1	
History storage period (in days)	90	
Trend storage period (in days)	365	
Store value	As is ▼	
Show value	As is ▼	show value mappings
Allowed hosts		

How it works

On the server side, we create a trapper item. A trapper item works as an active item the data has to be send to the server. For this we make use of the zabbix_sender tool.

To be able to get information from this zabbix_sender tool, we need to send with the -z option the IP of the Zabbix server together with hostname as registered in the Zabbix frontend (-s). We also need to tell our server what key we want to update (-k) and the value that we will give to this key (-o). There are plenty more options that we can specify like the port or a configuration file. Have a look at the `zabbix_sender` with the option -h or the Zabbix documentation for more information about them.

There's more...

If you have looked carefully, then you would have noticed that in our item there is an option **Allowed hosts**. As the trapper just accepts data from anywhere, it can be abused by someone if they know what key to use. This is not so hard to find out as the Zabbix protocol is not encrypted. So in production, it's probably a good idea to fill in this field with the IP from the hosts that is allowed to send information.

Another possibility is to send a text file to the Zabbix server with a list of hosts and the items with the values. If we create a file like this, then we have to put the name of the host first followed by the item key and the value, all separated by a space.

```
Ex: datafile.txt
server1 value1.key 10
server1 value2.key 20
server2 value2.key 10
server2 value2.key 20
```

We would then send this data with the `zabbix_sender` to our server. The command for this would look like this:

zabbix_sender -z <ip zabbix server> -i datafile.txt

More options can be found by running the `zabbix_sender -h` command.

In case of issues, you could make use of the option -vv.

If you make use of a proxy then the zabbix_sender needs to send its data to the proxy responsible for that host.

See also

- More information about the trapper item can be found here in the Zabbix documentation

  `https://www.zabbix.com/documentation/2.4/manual/config/items/itemtypes/trapper?s[]=trapper`

- Also have a look at the documentation of the `zabbix_sender`:

  `https://www.zabbix.com/documentation/2.4/manpages/zabbix_sender`

IPMI checks

We have already seen a few ways to monitor our infrastructure with Zabbix. One of the other supported methods of Zabbix is IPMI monitoring. If you still have no clue what we are talking about then maybe **ILO** or **DRAC** will tell you more. DRAC is from Dell and stands for **Dell Remote Access Controller** and ILO is from HP and stands for **Integrated Lights-out**. Most of these interfaces come in servers as extra cards, and make it possible for us to monitor our hardware directly without the need of an operating system. The server doesn't even need to be turned on to monitor the hardware.

Getting ready

For this topic, you need as usual a properly configured Zabbix server. Make sure you have compiled the server with support included for OpenIPMI. We also need some IPMI capable device, probably a server with a remote management card.

How to do it ...

1. First thing we need to do is go to our server and create a user for Zabbix in our IPMI device. It's wise to create on all servers, an extra user just for Zabbix instead of making use of the administrator account as Zabbix only needs read access.

2. Make sure IPMI tool is installed and OpenIPMI. This can be done by running:

   ```
   yum install impitool OpenIPMI OpenIPMI-libs
   ```

3. We can test our access to the IPMP interface with the next command:

   ```
   ipmitool -U <ipmi user> -H <IP of ipmi host> -I lanplus -L
   User sensor
   ```

4. When we run this command, we need to enter our password and the IPMI interface will return us some similar output (this is the output from a **HP ML350 G5** server).

```
UID Light       | 0x0     | discrete  | 0x0080| na       | na       | na
Int. Health LED | 0x0     | discrete  | 0x0080| na       | na       | na
Ext. Health LED | 0x0     | discrete  | 0x0080| na       | na       | na
Power Supply 1  | 0x0     | discrete  | 0x0180| na       | na       | na
Power Supply 2  | 0x0     | discrete  | 0x0180| na       | na       | na
Power Supplies  | 0x0     | discrete  | 0x0180| na       | na       | na
VRM 1           | 0x0     | discrete  | 0x0280| na       | na       | na
VRM 2           | 0x0     | discrete  | 0x0280| na       | na       | na
Fan Block 1     | 34.888  | percent   | ok    | na       | na       | na
Fan Block 2     | 29.792  | percent   | ok    | na       | na       | na
Fan Block 3     | 37.240  | percent   | ok    | na       | na       | na
Fan Blocks      | 0x0     | discrete  | 0x0180| na       | na       | na
Temp 1          | 41.000  | degrees C | ok    | 0.000    | 0.000    | 0.000
Temp 2          | 17.000  | degrees C | ok    | 0.000    | 0.000    | 0.000
Temp 3          | 34.000  | degrees C | ok    | 0.000    | 0.000    | 0.000
Temp 4          | 34.000  | degrees C | ok    | 0.000    | 0.000    | 0.000
Temp 5          | 26.000  | degrees C | ok    | 0.000    | 0.000    | 0.000
Temp 6          | 34.000  | degrees C | ok    | 0.000    | 0.000    | 0.000
Temp 7          | 34.000  | degrees C | ok    | 0.000    | 0.000    | 0.000
Power Meter     | 362     | Watts     | ok    | na       | na       | na
```

5. Next we need to configure our Zabbix server. For this, we have to go to the host interface. Remember this can be found under **Configuration | Host**.

6. Under **IPMI Interfaces**, add the correct **IP address** of the IPMP interface with the correct **Port**.

7. When this is done, go to the tab **IPMI** on the same page and fill in all the fields:

    1. **Authentication algorithm** in our case can stay `Default`.

    2. **Privilege level** in our case can stay `User`.

    3. For **Username** and **Password**, we need to fill in the username and password created in the IPMI interface for Zabbix. As you can see, the password is visible to everybody with administration rights.

4. Don't forget to click the **Update** button when you are finished.

8. The next step is to create a Zabbix item. As usual, we first fill in the name of our item.

9. As **Type** we select `IPMIagent`.

10. Make sure that the **Host interface** is the correct one that points to our IPMI.

11. For the **IPMI Sensor**, we can select one of the sensors that the IPMI returned when we checked it with our IPMI tool. The name must be exactly the same as returned by the IPMI tool.

12. The rest of the information depends on the item that you want to monitor; in this case, the returned **Type of information** is a float and since we measure the temperature, it makes sense to tell Zabbix that the **Units** are in degree celsius.

13. Our first item is ready so you can click the **Add** button at the bottom.

Last thing that we have to change is in the `zabbix_server.conf` file. Here we have to uncomment `StartIPMIPollers=0` and change the `0` in a value high enough to the number of IPMI devices that we want to monitor.

14. When this is done, restart the Zabbix server which can be done with:

`service zabbix-server restart.`

Passwords and pass phrases should not be shown in the frontend so please remind Zabbix about this by voting on this issue!
`https://support.zabbix.com/browse/ZBXNEXT-2461.`
It is best to open the IPMI with the latest firmware available if possible. Your IPMI device should at least support IPMI v2.0.

How it works

Getting IPMI to work is not too difficult but we need to make sure that our server is compiled with OpenIPMI support and that all packages are installed with a version of at least 2.0.14.

By default Zabbix is not configured to start any IPMI pollers, so in our server configuration file, we need to make sure that the IPMI pollers option is active and that enough pollers are set to monitor our IPMI devices. Don't forget to restart the server afterwards.

The IPMI device itself needs to have support for IPMI v2.0. Zabbix needs a user with read access on the IPMI so that it can read the data from the IPMI interface.

In Zabbix we need to make sure that on the host we add an extra interface for IPMI.

In the **host** tab of our server we need to add an IPMI interface here we need to configure the correct IP address and port.

There's more...

Zabbix has reported that the OpenIPMI version 2.0.7 is broken and that at least version 2.0.14 is needed to get a working version.

It is possible that your network card also supports IPMI. In this case there is no extra network card and you just have to fill in the same IP address for the IPMI interface.

More sensors can be found by placing Zabbix in debug level 4 and looking for the `reading_type` parameter. More information about sensors can be found in the IPMI specifications.

`http://www.intel.com/content/www/us/en/servers/ipmi/ipmi-specifications.html.`

See also

▸ As always check the latest Zabbix documentation for updates on IPMI monitoring:

`https://www.zabbix.com/documentation/2.4/manual/config/items/itemtypes/ipmi`

JMX checks

Since Zabbix 2.0, there is native support for monitoring Java applications in Zabbix. For this, Zabbix makes use of a so-called Java gateway. Once the gateway is in place, Zabbix can monitor all JMX counters from our Java application.

Getting ready

For this setup to work, you need as usual, your Zabbix server setup and access with full administration rights. We also need a host configured in Zabbix that we can use to install our JMX and Java application. If you have compiled your server from source, then make sure you have compiled it with the `--enable-java` option.

How to do it...

1. First thing to do on our Zabbix server is to install the Java gateway. This can be done with the following command:

   ```
   yum install zabbix-java-gateway
   ```

2. Make the Java gateway start up automatic next reboot:

   ```
   chkconfig zabbix-java-gateway on
   ```

   For RHEL 7:

   ```
   systemctl enable zabbix-java-gateway
   ```

3. Start the Java gateway:

   ```
   service start zabbix-java-gateway
   ```

   For RHEL 7:

   ```
   systemctl start zabbix-java-gateway
   ```

4. In the `zabbix_server.conf` file, change the following options:

   ```
   Java gateway = 127.0.0.1
   Java Gateway Port = 10052
   Start Java pollers = 2
   ```

5. Don't forget to restart your `zabbix-server`:

   `service zabbix-server restart`

   For RHEL 7:

   `systemctl restart zabbix-server`

6. There is a `zabbix-java-gateway.conf` file as well, where you can specify the same parameters to update this file.

7. Now you need to enable the JMX interface on the application on your host. This you have to do per application as the JMX interface usually comes disabled. Example:

```
java -Dcom.sun.management.jmxremote \
-Dcom.sun.management.jmxremote.port = 12345 \
-Dcom.sun.management.jmxremote.authenticate = True \
-Dcom.sun.management.jmxremote.ssl = True \
-jar some-java-app.jar
```

8. Another solution could be to add this to the configuration file of your application.

9. The next step is to create the JMX interface on our host in Zabbix.

| JMX interfaces | ↕ | 192.168.10.107 | | IP DNS | 12345 | ⦿ | Remove |
| Add | | | | | | | |

10. As the last step, create your item on the host and give it a proper **Name**.

11. The **Type** this time will be `JMX agent`.

12. Add the JMX item you would like to be monitored in the **Key** field.

13. Select the proper **Host interfaces**.

Item	
Name	Java CPU Usage
Type	JMX agent ▼
Key	jmx[java.lang:type=OperatingSystem,ProcessCpuLoad] Select
Host interface	192.168.10.107 : 12345 ▼
User name	
Password	
Type of information	Numeric (float) ▼
Units	%

14. Don't forget to open the proper ports in your firewall.

15. Go check the latest data page for your data.

There's more...

As you will see, JMX monitoring is not a straightforward thing. Sometimes your application won't connect to the correct IP or a type will refuse the Java to start.

On top of that, installing the JMX console will be a security risk. Luckily enough, we can add a login and a password to this console and Zabbix has support for this. In our item, there is a box where we can add a login and a password.

If you run into issues and you probably will, the best thing to do is to go and check the `jmx log` files under:

```
/var/log/zabbix_java_gateway.log
```

> Only one Java gateway can be installed on the Zabbix server or alternatively you could install one per proxy.
>
> When you compile it may be a good idea to add some prefix for the location, as the gateway comes with a whole tree of files and directories. Example:
>
> ```
> --prefix=/opt/zabbix_java_gateway
> ```

See also

- https://www.zabbix.com/documentation/2.4/manual/config/items/itemtypes/jmx_monitoring
- https://www.zabbix.com/documentation/2.4/manual/concepts/java

Aggregate checks

Running individual checks has been great so far, but they are just checks on one system. What if you would like to know the total CPU load of a group of servers? For example, when you are running a cluster of servers? For this we can make use of the aggregated checks in Zabbix.

Getting ready

To be able to finish this recipe successfully we need our Zabbix server with a few Linux hosts installed and properly configured.

How to do it ...

1. First, we create a new host called `linuxgroup`, for the agent IP address we can just put `0.0.0.0` and add it in a fictive hostgroup or for example, **Discovered hosts**.

2. Next, we create a new group (**Configuration | Host groups**) "`aggregated`" and we add two or more Linux hosts in this group.

3. Now we create an active item "`system.cpu.load[percpu,avg1]`" in a new template that we can link to all our hosts available in our "`aggregated`" group.

4. The next step is to create a new template for example `aggregated-linux` and link this template to our fake host `linuxgroup` that we made in step 1.

5. In this template, create an item with the **Key**:

   `grpavg["aggregated","system.cpu.load[percpu,avg1]","last"," 0"]`

Item	
Parent items	aggregated-linux
Name	AVG CPU Load for $1
Type	Zabbix aggregate
Key	grpavg["aggregated","system.cpu.load[percpu,avg1]","last","0"]
Type of information	Numeric (float)
Units	
Use custom multiplier	☐ 1
Update interval (in sec)	30
Flexible intervals	**Interval** **Period** **Action** No flexible intervals defined.
New flexible interval	Interval (in sec) 50 Period 1-7,00:00-24:00 Add
History storage period (in days)	90
Trend storage period (in days)	365
Store value	As is
Show value	As is show value mappings

When you go now to **Monitoring | Latest data**, you will see on our fake host the average CPU load from all our hosts in the group "`aggregated`".

	Name ↑	Last check	Last value
	- other - (1 Item)		
	AVG CPU Load for aggregated	2014-09-22 19:44:47	0.03

(LATEST DATA — Items; Host groups: type here to search [Select]; Hosts: linuxgroup [Select]; Application: [Select]; Name: ; Show items without data: ☑; Show details: ☐; [Filter] [Reset])

How it works

Aggregated items summarize the readings of an item of all hosts in a group together. The structure used to create an aggregated item is as follows:

```
groupfunc["Host group","Item key",itemfunc,timeperiod]
```

The `groupfunc` is just a placeholder and needs to be replaced with `grpavg`, `grpmax`, `grpmin`, or `grpsum`. The `Host group` is the group of servers that we want to use for our calculation. The item key is the item that is available on all servers in the group. The item function can be `avg`, `count`, `last`, `max`, `min`, or `sum`.

There's more...

Aggregated checks don't rely on any Zabbix agent or server check. Instead the Zabbix server will look at existing data in the database and reuse it to calculate a new item.

When you create an aggregated check in a template and link this template to all servers in for example, the group `webservers`; then Zabbix will recalculate this check on every server in this group. The result is that Zabbix server will calculate and store the same data for every server. One solution is to add the item local on a host or a better solution could be to create a fake host like we did in the example with the name related to the purpose of our cluster.

> Only active items on enabled hosts are included in the calculations.
>
> The amount of values (prefixed with #) is not supported.
>
> The time period parameter is ignored by the server if the third parameter (item function) is last.

See also

> ▶ https://www.zabbix.com/documentation/2.4/manual/config/items/
> itemtypes/aggregate

External checks

Just when you thought things couldn't get any better, you notice that Zabbix has support for external checks. This means that Zabbix will run a script or a binary from a specific location, without the need of any agent running on the host that we want to monitor.

Getting ready

For this setup, we need our Zabbix server with a host that can be reached by the Zabbix server. There is no need to install a Zabbix agent on the host as we will make use of our own scripts to run some checks.

How to do it ...

1. Creating external checks is very easy in Zabbix. First thing we need to verify is where to put them on our Zabbix server. This can be done by looking in the configuration file of the Zabbix server in the `zabbix_server.conf` file. Here we see the option `ExternalScripts` where we can specify the location or use the standard one:

   ```
   ExternalScripts=/usr/lib/zabbix/externalscripts
   ```

2. In this location, we will place our script. For example we could check the number of cores available on our host. So let's create a script `cores.sh` with the following content:

   ```
   #!/bin/bash
   nproc
   ```

3. Next step is to make our script executable; this can be done by the command:

   ```
   chmod +x
   ```

4. Next we need to make it accessible by our Zabbix server. Remember Zabbix runs as user `zabbix` and group `zabbix` so we need to change the user and the group.

   ```
   chown zabbix:zabbix cores.sh
   ```

5. Next step is to create our item for the host that we want to check.

6. For the **Name**, we put something that links us with the item we want to monitor such as `Number of CPU Cores`.

7. Then we select for **Type**, `External check`.

8. The **Key** is the name of our script; in our case `cores.sh[]`.

9. The values that we get back is numeric and decimal so **Type of information** and **Data type** can be left as is, together with all other options.

Item

Name	Number of CPU Cores
Type	External check ▼
Key	cores.sh[] Select
Host interface	192.168.10.102 : 10050 ▼
Type of information	Numeric (unsigned) ▼
Data type	Decimal ▼
Units	
Use custom multiplier	☐ 1
Update interval (in sec)	30
Flexible intervals	**Interval** **Period** **Action**
	No flexible intervals defined.
New flexible interval	Interval (in sec) 50 Period 1-7,00:00-24:00 Add

How it works

This example was pretty easy, but it should give you an idea of the possibilities of external checks. It's important that our scripts are placed in the correct directory as defined in our `zabbix_server.conf` file and that the script has the correct rights, so that Zabbix can read and execute the script.

Next step is to create an item in Zabbix and select the **Type**, `External check` and add a key with the exact same name as our script.

There's more...

It is important to remember that external checks cannot take too much time to run. If a script takes more than 5 seconds, Zabbix will then mark the item as unsupported.

If your scripts needs input such as a variable then you can pass this variable in your item key between the `[]`. For example, `myscript.sh["var1","var2",...]`.

It is also possible to make use of macros. For example, running a script that sends the IP address with some variable could be done easily like this:

```
myscript.sh["{HOST.IP}","var1"]
```

If you monitor your host from a proxy, then you need to make sure that the script is on the proxy that the host monitors. In that case, it will be the proxy running the script.

See also

▸ https://www.zabbix.com/documentation/2.4/manual/config/items/itemtypes/external

Database monitoring

In Zabbix when we want to monitor some database, it is possible to do this by making use of the **Open Database Connectivity** (**ODBC**) software. ODBC is kind of a software sitting between the DBMS and the application (in our case Zabbix). Zabbix can query any database, which is supported by **unixODBC** or **Independent Open DataBase Connectivity** (**iODBC**).

Getting ready

We need of course, our Zabbix server setup. If you have compiled the server then you need to make sure that it was compiled with the option `--with-unixODBC`.

How to do it...

1. Make sure you have the packages installed for ODBC on our CentOS / Red Hat; it can be done by installing the `unixODBC` packages.

   ```
   # yum install unixODBC  -y
   # yum install unixODBC-devel -y (if you need sources to
   compile)
   ```

2. Next, we need a proper connector for our database. In our case the database is MySQL. If you have another database, look for the specific connector for your database:

   ```
   # yum install mysql-connector-odbc
   ```

3. Next we need to configure the `odbcinst.ini` file. Here we have to add the location of our ODBC database driver. To find the location you can run the next command:

   ```
   # odbcinst -j
   unixODBC 2.2.14
   DRIVERS............: /etc/odbcinst.ini
   SYSTEM DATA SOURCES: /etc/odbc.ini
   ```

4. So we can now to edit the line `odbcinst.ini` and list our database driver:

```
# vi /etc/odbcinst.ini


# Driver from the mysql-connector-odbc package
# Setup from the unixODBC package
[MySQL]
Description     = ODBC for MySQL
Driver          = /usr/lib/libmyodbc5.so
Setup           = /usr/lib/libodbcmyS.so
Driver64        = /usr/lib64/libmyodbc5.so
Setup64         = /usr/lib64/libodbcmyS.so
FileUsage       = 1
```

This file should already be OK, just make sure that the library for the `Driver64` option is really on the system in that location.

1. Edit the `odbc.ini` file to create our `dsn` (data source) and add our database `config.`:

```
# vi /etc/odbc.ini
[mysql-test] => name of the dsn we will use
Description = Mysql test DB
Driver = mysql
Server = 127.0.0.1
User = root
Password = <root db password>
Port = 3306
Database = <zabbix database>
```

2. Now let's see if we can make a connection with our database:

```
# isql mysql-test
```

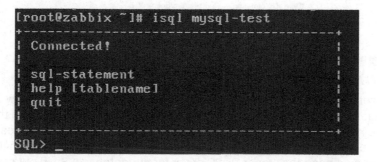

3. The output should look like this, if you have an error, check all of the above again for typos. Another solution could be to run `isql` command with the `-v` option for verbose.

4. Now it's time to go to Zabbix and create a new item on our host. **Configuration | Hosts | Items | Create item**.

5. For the **Name**, we just add a name easy for us to remember what item it is.

6. **Type** is where we select `Database monitor`.

7. **Key** is already filled in. We just need to replace the `<unique short description>` with our own unique key naming and `<dsn>` with our DSN name from the one in the `odbc.ini` file.

8. We don't need to fill in username and password as we added it in the `odbc.ini` file already.

9. **SQL query** is the field where we can put our SQL query that we want to run on our database. In our case, we added `select count(*) from items`.

10. **Type of information** is in our case `Numeric`.

11. **Data type** for us is `Decimal`.

12. Now go to **Latest data** page and see as data comes in after some time if all went well.

Item	
Name	MySQL Test DB
Type	Database monitor ▼
Key	db.odbc.select[my-mysql-test,mysql-test] Select
User name	
Password	
SQL query	select count(*) from items
Type of information	Numeric (unsigned) ▼
Data type	Decimal ▼

How it works

To be able to get Zabbix to read data from our database, we need to keep a few simple steps in mind. We need to compile Zabbix with UnixODBC support for which we need the package `unixODBC-devel`. Zabbix does not connect directly to the database but makes use of ODBC for this so we need to install the `unixODBC` package as well. Depending on what database we want to use, we also need the proper ODBC driver for our database. So in our case we had to make use of the `mysql-connector-odbc` package.

Next, we had to configure unixODBC which was done by editing two files odbcinst.ini and odbc.ini. The odbcinst.ini file is used to configure the installed drivers. It seems Red Hat / Centos comes already with a basic configuration, so we didn't have to make any changes.

Next, we had to add a data source in the odbc.ini file which is what we call a DSN. The DSN name is always between [] and we need this name for our Zabbix item. We also had to add the driver, in our case, mysql- the server where our database was running and connection settings such as username, password, port, and database name.

There's more...

In our case, it was easy to install the MySQL driver because it was already provided in a package from our OS. Sometimes it's not so easy to find the correct driver for instance when using Oracle. The website from unixODBC has a list of supported databases and drivers: http://www.unixodbc.org/drivers.html.

Some limitations to keep in mind:

- ▶ The SQL command must begin with the select command.
- ▶ The SQL command may not include line breaks.
- ▶ The query can return only a single value.
- ▶ If the query returns more than one column, only the first column of Zabbix is considered.
- ▶ If the query returns more than one row only the first line is read.
- ▶ Queries can but must not be terminated with a semicolon.
- ▶ Macros are not replaced.
- ▶ The SQL command must start with sql= in lowercase.
- ▶ If the database is loaded, the response can come with a delay.
- ▶ Proxies if compiled also need the option – with -unixODBC.
- ▶ Every time a query runs, it executes a login.

See also

- ▶ https://www.zabbix.com/documentation/2.4/manual/config/items/itemtypes/odbc_checks

Checks with SSH

Another way to extend our Zabbix server to do some checks is by making use of **Secure Shell** (**SSH**). SSH checks will be launched from the server with the need of a Zabbix Agent.

Getting ready

For this example, we just need a Zabbix server properly configured and a host that we can use to connect to by making use of SSH.

How to do it...

When you log in with SSH, you have to provide a username and a password in Zabbix to log in to the host that we want to monitor. This must be done in the GUI in plain text. An alternative to this is the use of SSH keys.

1. The first thing we have to do in the `Zabbix_server.conf` file is to look for the option `SSHKeyLocation` and enable it and add a path for the location of our SSH key files. Add the following line to the `config` file.

    `SSHKeyLocation=/home/zabbix/.ssh`

2. First edit the `/etc/passwd` file and give a home folder to the user `zabbix`:

    `zabbix:x:500:500::/home/zabbix:/sbin/nologin`

3. Next, create the directory on the server. This can be done by running the following command:

    `# mkdir -p /home/zabbix/.ssh`

4. Next, give the correct rights to the folders and sub-folders:

    `# chown -R zabbix:zabbix /home/zabbix/`

5. Now restart the Zabbix server so that the new configuration is loaded:

    `# service zabbix-server restart`

    For RHEL 7:

    `# systemctl restart zabbix-server`

6. Now we can create a new pair of SSH keys for Zabbix:

    `# sudo -u zabbix ssh-keygen -t rsa -b 2048`

7. When the `keygen` option asks you for a pass-phrase, you can just press enter for none.

8. Now copy our key to the host that we want to monitor (this has to be done for every host we want to monitor if making use of SSH).

```
# sudo -u zabbix ssh-copy-id root@<host ip>
The authenticity of host '192.168.10.102 (192.168.10.102)' can't
be established.

RSA key fingerprint is 2f:83:7f:0e:4b:bd:1b:6c:b7:b7:c4:69
:f6:99:10:71.

Are you sure you want to continue connecting (yes/no)? yes

Warning: Permanently added '192.168.10.102' (RSA) to the list of
known hosts.

root@192.168.10.102's password:

Now try logging into the machine, with "ssh
'root@192.168.10.102'", and check in:


   .ssh/authorized_keys


to make sure we haven't added extra keys that you weren't
expecting.
```

9. Now it should be possible to log in with our SSH key to the host without making use of a password:

```
# sudo -u zabbix ssh root@<ip host>
```

10. If this works, we are ready to create our item. On our host, add an item and give it a **Name**.

11. Next for **Type** select `SSH agent`.

12. Replace the **Key** with `ssh.run[test]` where test is just a unique name for our key.

13. As **Authentication method** we select `Public key` as we want to make use of our SSH key that we have created.

14. Since we copied our key to the host as user `root`, we will add `root` in the **User name** field.

15. In the box where we have to put **Public key file**, we add the name of our public key: `id_rsa.pub`.

16. In the field for the **Private key file**, we put our private key: `id_rsa`.

17. Next, we have a box **Executed script**; this box is the place where we can put the command that we want to launch on our host. For this example, we will put the next command to read the OS name from our host:

```
# head -n1 /etc/issue
```

18. The **Type of information** field can be `Text` as we will get a string back from the host:

Item	
Name	Check Issue
Type	SSH agent ▼
Key	ssh.run[test] Select
Host interface	192.168.10.102 : 10050 ▼
Authentication method	Public key ▼
User name	root
Public key file	id_rsa.pub
Private key file	id_rsa
Key passphrase	
Executed script	head -n1 /etc/issue
Type of information	Text ▼
Update interval (in sec)	30

19. Now save the item and go to **Monitoring | Latest data** to check your result:

⊟	issue (1 Item)		
☐	Check Issue	2014-09-23 18:13:33	CentOS release 6.5 (Final)

 Sometimes logging in with SSH may not work. In that case, check SELinux as SELinux is sometimes blocking SSH logins with keys because of incorrect labels on the SSH keys.

How it works

Zabbix will be configured as a normal user, we will give Zabbix a home directory under `/home/zabbix`. Here we will install our SSH keys for the Zabbix user. In the `zabbix_server.conf` file we have to specify this location, so our server knows where to look.

Next, we have to create an item for SSH and this item has to know the name of our private and public SSH keys.

It's important that we log in the first time manually ourselves on all the hosts so that the key is accepted on all the machines. This way we are also sure that SSH passwordless login works.

Now when Zabbix wants to launch the command that we added in the script box, it will be launched as the user that we told Zabbix to use to log in on the remote host.

There's more

Make sure that port 22 is not blocked in your firewall. Normally RHEL and derivatives have port 22 standard open in the firewall. If you use SSH on another port than the standard port 22, you need to specify this in your key parameters. Example. `ssh.run[<unique short description>,<ip>,<port>,<encoding>]`.

If you see messages in the log file like this:

```
<hostname> became not supported: Cannot obtain authentication
methods: Would block requesting userauth list
```

Then you have to check your DNS. This is probably a problem of SSH doing a hostname look-up without success. It can be fixed easily by adding the correct entry in the DNS or host file of the Zabbix server.

It takes more time and resources to check SSH items than to check them by making use of the agent. So don't be too aggressive with the check interval of the item.

See also

▶   https://www.zabbix.com/documentation/2.4/manual/config/items/itemtypes/ssh_checks

Checks with Telnet

In this setup, we will see how to set up a check with Telnet and Zabbix. I personally don't see any reason for using Telnet anymore these days as there are plenty of other secure alternatives (Example, SSH). But just for the sys admin who likes to live on the edge or for the sys admin that has no other choice because of a company policy, this is it. (Remember that Telnet is not encrypted, so everybody can read your data!)

Getting ready

To make this setup work, all we need is a properly setup Zabbix server and a host with or without Zabbix agent as the check is initiated by the Zabbix server.

How to do it...

1. First on the host we need to be sure that we can connect with Telnet so we have to install a Telnet server. This can be done by running the next command:

    ```
    # yum -y install telnet-server
    ```

2. On the Zabbix server, we have to install Telnet, of course. This can be done by running the `install telnet` command:

```
# yum -y install telnet
```

3. Back on our client we have to edit the `xinet.d` file. For Telnet, this file can be found under the `/etc/xinit.d/` file. Here we have to change `disabled = yes` to `no`:

```
# vi /etc/xinetd.d/telnet
{
        flags           = REUSE
        socket_type     = stream
        wait            = no
        user            = root
        server          = /usr/sbin/in.telnetd
        log_on_failure  += USERID
        disable         = no
}
```

4. Now we have to activate the `xinetd` service.

```
# service xinetd start
```

5. And we need to make sure that the service starts automatically the next time we reboot:

```
# chkconfig telnet on

# chkconfig xinetd on
```

6. Next step that we have to take care of is the firewall. We need to make sure that port 23 is open so that we can connect with Telnet to our server.

```
# vi /etc/sysconfig/iptables

# Firewall configuration written by system-config-firewall

# Manual customization of this file is not recommended.

*filter

:INPUT ACCEPT [0:0]

:FORWARD ACCEPT [0:0]

:OUTPUT ACCEPT [0:0]

-A INPUT -m state --state ESTABLISHED,RELATED -j ACCEPT

-A INPUT -p icmp -j ACCEPT

-A INPUT -i lo -j ACCEPT

-A INPUT -p udp -m state --state NEW --dport 23 -j ACCEPT

-A INPUT -p tcp -m state --state NEW --dport 23 -j ACCEPT
```

```
-A INPUT -m state --state NEW -m tcp -p tcp --dport 22 -j ACCEPT
-A INPUT -j REJECT --reject-with icmp-host-prohibited
-A FORWARD -j REJECT --reject-with icmp-host-prohibited
COMMIT


If you run RHEL 7.X then the firewall ports can be added this way:
firewall-cmd --permanent --add-port=23/tcp
firewall-cmd --permanent --add-port=23/udp
firewall-cme --reload
```

7. After we have added the two lines in the firewall, we need to reload the firewall so that our adjustments become active:

    ```
    # service iptables restart
    ```

8. If we want to have access as `root` to our server, then we need to add an extra line in the file `/etc/securetty` at the end of the file:

    ```
    # vi /etc/securetty
    tty10
    tty11
    pts/0
    ```

9. In case you don't need to run your command as `root` you can create another user by running the command `useradd`:

    ```
    # useradd zabbix
    # passwd zabbix
    ```

10. Now we are ready to create our item in Zabbix. As always create the item in a template linked to our host or directly on the host.

11. First step is to give the item a **Name**.

12. Select `TELNET agent` as type from the list.

13. Modify the **Key** `telnet.run[<unique short description>,<ip>,<port>,<encoding>]` in `telnet.run[telnet.item]` where `telnet.item` is just a unique key name

14. Select the correct **Host interface**.

15. Fill in the **Username**.

16. Add the correct **Password**.

17. In the **Executed script** box, add your own script or like in our case something simple to test it, `Head -n1 /etc/issue`.

18. The **Type of information** box in this case will be `Text`.

Item	
Name	telnet item
Type	TELNET agent ▼
Key	telnet.run[telnet.item] Select
Host interface	192.168.10.102 : 10050 ▼
User name	telnet
Password	zabbix
Executed script	head -n1 /etc/issue
Type of information	Text ▼

19. Save your item and have a look at the latest data to see if your item works.

⊞	Security (2 Items)		
⊟	telnet (1 Item)		
	telnet item	2014-09-24 17:58:35	CentOS release 6.5 (Final)
⊞	Zabbix agent (3 Items)		

How it works

Just as with SSH, Zabbix server will initiate the connection to the host that we want to monitor. But because we work with Telnet, there is no secure way to log in and we have to add the login and password into the Zabbix item in plain text.

We have to install on the client, the Telnet server and we need to make sure that it is running and that it comes back up after a reboot.

It's also important that if you have a firewall running that we open the firewall on port 23 for TCP and UDP.

Keep in mind that standard our `root` user will not be allowed to initiate a connection. For this, we have to alter the file `/etc/securetty` first on the host.

Finally, if we make use of Telnet, we have to make sure that Telnet is installed on our Zabbix server so that we can initiate the connection.

Telnet is a protocol that is not encrypted, just like the Zabbix protocol. So when you use the `root` user to log into the host, remember that anyone will be able to sniff the `root` password from your network!

There's more...

If a Telnet check returns a value with non-ASCII characters and in non-UTF8 encoding, then the `<encoding>` parameter of the key should be properly specified.

Also remember, that if the script is resource intensive, it will cause delays in reporting to the server. Also Telnet checks are always more resource intensive than real agent checks.

See also

▸ https://www.zabbix.com/documentation/2.4/manual/config/items/itemtypes/telnet_checks

Calculated checks

Calculated items are items calculated based on data of one or more already existing items in the Zabbix database. All calculations are handled by the Zabbix server and will never be calculated on the agent or the proxy.

Getting ready

If you want to do this exercise, then you need a Zabbix server that is properly setup and linked to the standard Linux template. Of course, you can alter the items that we have used and use your own if you like.

How to do it...

1. The first step is to go to the Zabbix server and create a new item on the host or in a template.
2. Give the item a name, something such as `% free on root`.
3. Select the **Type**, `Calculated`.
4. Fill in the **Key** with a unique name, example `free.root`.
5. In the field **Formula**, we add:

   ```
   100*last("vfs.fs.size[/,free]",0)/last("vfs.fs.size[/,total
   ]",0)
   ```

6. Select `Numeric (float)` as **Type of information**.

7. And in the **Units** field, place `%`.

8. Those are the options we need to build our calculated item, so you can save it or give it an application first.

Item	
Name	% Free space on /
Type	Calculated ▼
Key	free.root
Formula	100*last("vfs.fs.size[/,free]",0)/last("vfs.fs.size[/,total]",0)
Type of information	Numeric (float) ▼
Units	%

9. Next we can go to **Monitoring | Latest data** to have a look at our new item.

Name ↑	Last check	Last value
Calculated (1 Item)		
% Free space on /	2014-09-25 18:26:35	60.44

How it works

A calculated item will calculate a new value from one or more items that already exist in the database. This means that the Zabbix server will calculate a new value of already existing data and create a new item for it.

In our case, we calculated the percentage of the free space on / by dividing the free space from our `root` filesystem with the total size from our `root` filesystem and then we multiplied the data hundred times. The last option in our example makes sure that we use only the latest data from our two items.

When we create calculated items, we always need a function, key and optionally some parameters:

```
func(<key>|<hostname:key>,<parameter1>,...)
```

There's more...

We can make use of many different functions and are not limited to just the latest data. For instance, we can make use of avg, count, max, min, sum, and so on.

For a complete overview, have a look at this page in the Zabbix documentation.

https://www.zabbix.com/documentation/2.4/manual/appendix/triggers/functions.

 We can only use calculated items on numeric values. Here is no support for strings as yet.

See also

▶ https://www.zabbix.com/documentation/2.4/manual/config/items/itemtypes/calculated

Building web scenarios

Now that we have seen plenty of ways to monitor all kinds of network devices, it's time to have a look at how we can monitor websites with Zabbix. With Zabbix, it's possible to monitor all kinds of information from web pages. In this recipe, we will explain you how to do it in a few easy steps.

Getting ready

Once again, we need our Zabbix server properly configured with a Zabbix super admin account. Make sure that the agent is installed on the Zabbix server and is working fine.

How to do it...

1. Go to **Configuration | Hosts** and click on the link web after your Zabbix host.
2. Click on the **Create scenario** button on the upper left side of the web page.
3. Give as **Name** for example, Zabbix availability check.
4. Create a new **Application** example, Zabbix web check.

5. Keep **Update interval**, **Retries** as is and select an **agent** example, **Firefox**.

6. In the field Variables, put the following data:

```
{user}=Admin
{password}="your zabbix Admin password"
```

Step 1: In this recipe, we will add the first step in our scenario to verify the existence of our front page.

1. Next click the tab **Steps** and click the **Add** button.

2. Give the first step a **Name** example, `Front page`.

3. Fill in the **URL** of the Zabbix front page (`http://localhost/zabbix/index.php`).

4. In the box **Required string** write `Zabbix SIA`.

5. And in the box **Required status codes**, we put the number `200`.

6. Now you can click the **Add** button to add our rule to the list:

Step 2: Now we add a second step to login in our Zabbix web page.

1. Now we add a new step to our web scenario to monitor if we can login.

2. Give our step a **Name** example: `Login step`.

3. Add the **URL** of the Zabbix login page again: `http://localhost/zabbix/index.php` in the **URL** field.

4. In the box **Post** add the following line:

   `name={user}&password={password}&enter=Sign in`

5. In the box **Variables** we write add the next line:

   `{sid}=regex:sid=([0-9a-z]{16})`

6. And we look again for the **Required status codes** `200`.

7. Press **Add** to add the step to our scenario:

Step of scenario	
Name	Login step
URL	http://localhost/zabbix/index.php
Post	name={user}&password={password}&enter=Sign in
Variables	{sid}=regex:sid=([0-9a-z]{16})
Headers	
Follow redirects	☑
Retrieve only headers	☐
Timeout	15
Required string	
Required status codes	200
	Add Cancel

Step 3: In our third,step we will verify if the login step that we just made actually works:

1. Next, we create yet another step to see if our login actually worked.

2. Give the step a **Name**, example, `Login check`.

3. Once again, fill in the correct URL in the **URL** field:

   `http://localhost/zabbix/index.php`

4. In the field **Required string**, we put the word `Profile`.

5. And in the **Required status code** field, we place `200` again:

Step of scenario	
Name	Login check
URL	http://localhost/zabbix/index.php
Post	
Variables	
Headers	
Follow redirects	✔
Retrieve only headers	☐
Timeout	15
Required string	Profile
Required status codes	200
	Add Cancel

6. Press **Add** to add our third step.

Step 4: In our fourth and last step we will log out of the web page to make sure all sessions are closed.

1. For this, we create a new step to see if we can log out.

2. Give our final step a **Name**, example, `Logout`.

3. Add the following URL in the `URL` field:

   `http://localhost/zabbix/index.php?reconnect=1&sid={sid}`

4. And fill in the **Required status codes** of `200`.

5. Press **Add** button to add our final step to the scenario.

Step of scenario	
Name	Logout
URL	http://localhost/zabbix/index.php?reconnect=1&sid={sid}
Post	
Variables	
Headers	
Follow redirects	☑
Retrieve only headers	☐
Timeout	15
Required string	
Required status codes	200
	Add Cancel

6. Make sure now that you save all steps and also the complete scenario in the first tab!

7. Go to **Monitoring | Web** and click on **Zabbix Availability Check**.

8. You will see if everything is fine; a table with **Speed, Response time**, and **Response code** for each step and below it, some graphs.

How it works

When we want to monitor websites, we have to create a scenario. This scenario is based on a certain level of steps. Each step will be executed in the exact the same order.

In our scenario, we have added some variables for user and password between { } so that we don't have to type our login and password every time in the other steps.

We then added a first step just to monitor the front page; here we filled in the code `200` in the required status codes field. A web server will always return a certain code when we open a web page `200` is the code for OK. More codes can be found here: `http://en.wikipedia.org/wiki/List_of_HTTP_status_codes`.

We also looked for a required string. This is a unique text on the web page that we see only when we are at the login page of our website.

In the next step, we tried to log in. For this we made use of the post and the variables boxes.

In the post box, we added the string that we need to post with our username and password. Remember we made macros for this. Be careful we have to enter everything in one line and have to glue it together with `&`. Also, in this example we make use of name and password for name and password but this can change. You have to look in the code of the web page what the exact post variables are. Same goes for the `enter=Sign` option in, this is the post variable used to enter the username and password.

The variables box is a regular expression that we need because the web page makes use of a session ID. We put our `regexp` option in a macro `{sid}` that we can use later.

In our third step, we are already logged in so the only thing to verify if login really worked is add a required string that can only be seen once you are logged in. In our case, that is the word `Profile`.

Now in our final step, we will try to log out, else all sessions will stay recorded in the database. In some cases it is possible that you can't log in for a certain amount of time because your session is still active.

For this, we have to add the URL that we need to log out and we also have to pass our session ID. Here we can make use of the `{sid}` macro that we made earlier in step 2.

There's more...

A few extra tips to keep in mind when you monitor websites:

- If you need to monitor a website that is not running on one of your Zabbix hosts, then the best way to do it is to create a dummy host and use this host to monitor the website.

- It is not possible to skip some steps; if one step fails the scenario will stop.

- There is no support at the moment for JavaScript in Zabbix web monitoring.

- Web monitoring has a hard-coded history of 30 days and a 90 days trend period.

- Since Zabbix 2.4, there is support in steps to follow web page redirects and to retrieve only the headers from web pages.

- Since Zabbix 2.4, it is possible to increase the log level only for a certain process. To debug issues with web monitoring, it can be handy to do this for the HTTP poller.

```
# zabbix_server -R log_level_increase="http poller"
```

See also

- https://www.zabbix.com/documentation/2.4/manual/web_monitoring

Monitoring web scenarios

Now that we have our website monitored, we have nice graphs about download speed, access times and so on. But sometimes there are certain things that we would like to know like when a step fails in our scenario. This recipe will show you how to monitor the same.

Getting ready

Make sure you have your Zabbix server properly configured, that you have super admin rights and that you have finished the previous recipe *Building web scenarios*.

How to do it...

1. Our first step is to go to **Configuration | Hosts** and click on the group **Triggers** on that host.

2. Add a new trigger to our host by clicking on the **Create trigger** button in the upper right corner.

3. Give a name to our new trigger in the **Name** field.

4. In the **Expression** box add the following line :

   `{host:web.test.fail[Scenario].last(0)}>0`

5. Don't forget to replace host with your host name or template name and Scenario with the name of your scenario.

6. Select the preferred severity level.

7. To save our trigger, click the **Add** button at the bottom.

Trigger	Dependencies

Name	Availability check
Expression	{Zabbix server:web.test.fail[Zabbix Availability Check].last(0)}>0 [Add]
	Expression constructor
Multiple PROBLEM events generation	☐
Description	
URL	
Severity	Not classified Information **Warning** Average High Disaster
Enabled	☑

[Update] [Clone] [Delete] [Cancel]

Zabbix 2.4.0 Copyright 2001-2014 by Zabbix SIA

8. In our web scenario replace for example, the password with a wrong password.

9. Go to the page **Monitoring | Triggers** and see your trigger going in alarm.

How it works...

Even if we did not create an item, it is still possible to monitor certain aspects of our web scenario. When we create our scenario Zabbix adds certain items by itself to our host. This way we can monitor certain aspects like for example, the number of failed steps.

Here we have an overview of the steps that can be monitored with Zabbix:

- `web.test.in [Scenario,,bps]`: Will monitor the download speed
- `web.test.fail[Scenario]`: Will monitor the failed steps
- `web.test.error[Scenario]`: Will monitor the error messages
- `web.test.time[Scenario,Step]`: Will monitor the response time
- `web.test.rspcode[Scenario,Step]`: Will monitor the response code

See also

- `https://www.zabbix.com/documentation/2.4/manual/web_monitoring/items`

Some advanced monitoring tricks

There are some more tricks that can be used when creating items and we have already made use of them in the book. So, maybe you have noticed it already and found out how it works. If not, we will show you now and explain you how it works.

Getting ready

For this recipe, we just need our Zabbix server up and running and access rights as super administrator. We also need to have our agent installed on our Zabbix server and properly configured.

How to do it ...

1. Let's take next recipe as example and change the **Name** in `Mac Address on $1`.
2. Now let's modify the **Key** and specify that we want the MAC address from `eth0` only `system.hw.macaddr[eth0,]`.

Item	
Name	Mac Address on $1
Type	Zabbix agent ▼
Key	system.hw.macaddr[eth0,] `Select`
Host interface	127.0.0.1 : 10050 ▼
Type of information	Text ▼
Update interval (in sec)	30

3. Now click the **Update** button.

4. Now go to the list with all items and take a look at your item. You will see that the name now is `Mac Address on eth0`.

How it works...

When we make use of the $ symbol in our item name, `$1` will be linked with the first value from our key. When our key has more than one value, let's say three values then we can make use of `$1`, `$2`, and `$3` to read those values.

This makes life more easy when we work with templates. For more information about templates go to *Chapter 6, Working with Templates* in Zabbix.

See also

▸ `https://www.zabbix.com/documentation/2.4/manual/config/items/item`

Autoinventory

Besides monitoring values to see if something goes wrong, Zabbix has another nice feature. It is possible to gather certain information of your hardware and use this to create some inventory in Zabbix. Knowing we have an API in Zabbix, it can be used to populate our **Configuration Management Database** (**CMDB**) later.

Getting ready

Make sure you have your Zabbix server up and running with super administrator rights. We can do this recipe with only the Zabbix server added as host; having said that, it won't hurt if you add a extra host to monitor the inventory from this machine.

How to do it ...

1. The first thing we do is go to **Configuration** | **Host** then click on the host that we want to configure.

2. Now click the **Host Inventory** button and select **Automatic** from the menu and press **Update**.

![Configuration of hosts screenshot showing Host Inventory tab with Automatic selected]

3. Now go to the menu to add a new item on the host or create a new template and create a new item in the template.

4. Give our item **Name** the name `Mac Address` as we are going to get the MAC address from our host.

5. As **Type**, we select `Zabbix agent`.

6. For the **Key** we select `system.hw.macaddr[]` from the list with keys.

7. Select the correct **Host interface**.

8. And select `Text` as **Type of information**.

9. Create a **New application** for example `Inventory`.

10. Now select the **Populates host inventory** field and select here `MAC address A` from the list.

11. Save the item and wait a bit so that our items gets updated.

12. Now go to the menu **Inventory | Hosts** and select from the right dropdown, the correct host.

13. If all went well, you will see the MAC address from your host in Zabbix.

![Host inventory screenshot showing the MAC address A field populated]

14. Now when you go back to **Configuration | Hosts** and you click on your host, you will see that in the tab **Host inventory**, the field `MAC address A` is populated.

How it works...

To get our inventory fields populated, we need to create items on our hosts. Those items have to be linked to fields from our inventory. Once the items are detected the data will be put in the inventory fields from our host. It's good practice to create a specific template to detect certain information that you need and apply the template to all your hosts.

There's more...

Be careful, not all items work on all operating systems. For instance, it is at times possible that one item works on Fedora and not on Ubuntu, example, OS short name. It is also possible to make use of macros in the reporting. A full list of macros can be found here:

```
https://www.zabbix.com/documentation/2.4/manual/appendix/macros/
supported_by_location.
```

We could make use of the macros {INVENTORY.LOCATION<1-9>} and {INVENTORY.CONTACT<1-9>} to get notified in case of issues with the location and the contact person for this server.

See also

 ▶ ```
    https://www.zabbix.com/documentation/2.4/manual/config/hosts/
    inventory
    ```
    ```

5

Testing with Triggers in Zabbix

In this chapter, we will cover the following topics:

- ▸ Creating triggers
- ▸ Monitoring log files
- ▸ Triggering constructor
- ▸ More advanced triggers
- ▸ Testing our trigger expressions

Introduction

So far we have seen how to install Zabbix, set it up and configure it. In *Chapter 4, Monitoring with Zabbix* we have shown you the different ways to gather data with Zabbix. The next logical step for us is now to check our data for certain values or thresholds that we are interested it. In this chapter, we will see how we can build our own triggers to get notified about certain thresholds and how to work with the trigger constructor in Zabbix. We will also see a more advanced way to build triggers and a way to test our expression before we go in production.

Creating triggers

Let us see first how to create our own triggers. Triggers in Zabbix are ways to check the data that we have gathered for certain thresholds. Later we can use this in Zabbix to send us notifications about certain thresholds that have been exceeded.

Getting ready

To be able to do this recipe, you need a Zabbix server with super administrator access such as the standard admin account that came with the installation. We also need a network device that we can monitor in Zabbix.

How to do it...

1. Our first step is to create a simple check. Our simple check will launch a ping command to our host. As host, you can choose any network device that is pingable. If you don't know how to do this, I suggest you go back to *Chapter 4, Monitoring with Zabbix* and run over the recipe *Simple checks*. Just a simple check will do. There is no need to add special options.

2. Go to your host. This can be done from the menu **Configuration | Hosts** and click there on **Triggers**.

3. Fill in the **Name** field, example .Zabbix agent on {HOST.NAME} is unreachable for 5 minutes. You see in the name {HOST.NAME}; this is a macro that will tell us the hostname when the trigger launches. This will make our life much easier when we get notified later about potential issues:

Trigger	Dependencies				

Name: Zabbix agent on {HOST.NAME} is unreachable for 5 minutes

Expression: {Host2:agent.ping.nodata(5m)}=1 [Add]

Expression constructor

Multiple PROBLEM events generation: ☐

Description:

URL:

Severity: | Not classified | Information | Warning | **Average** | High | Disaster |

Enabled: ☑

[Update] [Clone] [Delete] [Cancel]

4. Now it's time to write our expression {host:agent.ping.nodata(5m)}=1.

5. Host is the name of our host or the template that we use; then we place a : and after the : we place key with the function and optionally a parameter, `agent.ping.nodata(5m)`, and we end it with our operator or constant.

   `{<server>:<key>.<function>(<parameter>)}<operator><constant>`

6. Now when we look at the Zabbix dashboard **Monitoring | Dashboard**, we will see in the list with last 20 issues the warning that our Zabbix agent on host2 is down for more than 5 minutes.

How it works

In Zabbix when we create an item, we gather certain data from our network. For this we make use of different methods. In our case, we used the simple check to do a ping to an agent. When we want to get notified, we need to tell Zabbix when one of those values is an issue. In other words, we need to tell Zabbix what the threshold is. In our case, it was the value 0. So triggers are some kind of logical expression evaluating the data that we have gathered by our item.

The option **Multiple PROBLEM events generation** will generate an event in Zabbix every time the trigger evaluates a problem. Else only 1 event will be generated. The description field is helpful to add a description so that the person receiving the alarm will have a clue of what is going on. So it's best to put some meaningful description here. The URL field can be used to send, for example, a URL to a solution webpage. Severity is where we can select the severity level of our trigger. Enabled box speaks for itself; we can enable or disable our trigger here. The tab **Dependencies** on top can be used to link our trigger to other triggers. This way our trigger will not warn us in case the other trigger is not in a problem state.

There's more...

As extra, we added the option **nodata(5m)**. This option tells Zabbix to look for our date and warn us if there is no data for 5 minutes. We could replace the 5m with 300. This would be the same as Zabbix would calculate the time in seconds.

If you have issues with ping always returning the value 0. Check SELinux as SELinux is probably blocking Zabbix from using `fping` option.

One solution for this problem can be:

```
#grep fping /var/log/audit/audit.log | audit2allow -M zabbix_fping
#semodule -i zabbix_fping.pp
```

See also

▶   There is more than just the nodata option. More information about those options can be found on the Zabbix website:

    `https://www.zabbix.com/documentation/2.4/manual/config/triggers`.

▶   Also for the macro, other macros can be used. For example, we can make use of the $1 to display the constant of our expression. Also the macro **{HOST.NAME}**, could be replaced with another macro. For example, we could make use of **$1** to display the constant of our expression in our trigger name.

▶   In our case, $1 could be used to tell us that the value of `ping` was 0.

    `https://www.zabbix.com/documentation/2.4/manual/config/triggers/trigger`.

Testing log files

One of the many other things Zabbix can do is monitor log files. In this recipe, we will show you how to test your log files with Zabbix for certain patterns.

Getting ready

For this recipe, we need a Zabbix server without agent installed on the server and configured. We also need Zabbix super administrator access.

How to do it ...

Let's say we want to monitor the `/var/log/messages` file on our OS.

1.   First thing we need to do is make sure Zabbix has access to the file:

    ```
    # ll /var/log/messages
    -rw-------. 1 root root 324715 Jan 20 18:54 /var/log/messages
    ```

2.   As we can see, only the user `root` has read and write access to this file.

3.   Our next step is to add Zabbix to a new group example, `adm`; then later we can give this group access to our log file:

    ```
    # usermod -a -G adm zabbix
    ```

4.   Next step is to make the file readable for the group:

    ```
    # chmod g+r /var/log/messages
    ```

5.   Now we only have to add the file messages to the group `adm`:

    ```
    # chgrp adm /var/log/messages
    ```

6. Now when we check, our permissions should look like this on the `/var/log/messages` file:

```
# ll /var/log/messages
-rw-r-----. 1 root adm 327617 Jan 20 19:11 /var/log/messages
```

7. Our next step is to add an item in our Zabbix server to monitor this file. Go to **Configuration | Hosts |** and select **Item** for our Zabbix server. (Or better still, add it to a template that is linked to our Zabbix server).

8. Click **Create item** to create a new item.

9. Give a new **Name** to our item, example, `Errors in /var/log/messages`.

10. Select `Zabbix agent (active)` as **Type**.

11. Add the following **Key**: `log[/var/log/messages,error]`.

12. **Type of information** should be `Log`.

13. **Update interval** can be set to `1`.

14. Now save your item.

15. On the Zabbix server console, type:

```
# logger error
```

16. This will generate an error in our log file, so we can go now to **Configuration | Latest data** and look how the log file was monitored by our Zabbix server.

17. Create a Trigger so that we would be alarmed. We go to **Configuration | Hosts | Triggers** and click on **Create trigger**.

18. Give a descriptive name.

19. Add the following expression : `{<template or server>:log[/var/log/messages,error].logsource(error)}=0` so that you get notifications when we get errors in the `/var/log/messages` file.

Trigger	Dependencies	
Name	Errors in /var/log/messages	
Expression	{Template App Zabbix Server:log[/var/log/messages,error].logsource(error)}=0	Add
	Expression constructor	

There's more...

SELinux could be messing with you; so make sure to temporarily disable SELinux to make sure that this is not the problem. In case it is, a rule should be created for this.

The problem with logfile monitoring is that entries in log files do not have a status. If an entry in the log file indicates an error, there is usually no entry indicating that the error has been corrected. So in this case, the trigger will always retain the status error. We have to force Zabbix to update the status and this can be done with the nodata() function. In this case, we have to rewrite our previous trigger like this:

```
{<template or host>:log[/var/log/messages,error].nodata(300)}=0
```

In this case, we get an alarm when there is an error in the log file and Zabbix will reset it's status after 120 seconds:

Trigger	Dependencies	
Name	Errors in /var/log/messages	
Expression	{Template App Zabbix Server:log[/var/log/messages,error].nodata(120)}=0	Add
	Expression constructor	

In case you want to work with `logrotate` option, it is very much possible with Zabbix, except that we would have to use `logrt` option instead of `log` option.

How it works

Zabbix can look in files for certain keywords; for this, Zabbix needs to have read permissions on those files. In this example, we added Zabbix to the adm group. Then we added our log file to this group and gave the group read permissions. Now by creating the proper item, Zabbix was able to look into the file for out keyword error. With the command logger, we were able to send the command error to our log file and Zabbix picked it up.

Later we saw how it was possible to create the correct trigger for this, and what the possible problem could be with the entry not having a status. To solve this problem, we made use of the nodata function. This function makes it possible for Zabbix to monitor our log file and reset it's status back to normal if no new errors were received for 300 seconds. Of course, in this case you need to be sure that Zabbix is configured to send email, SMS, and so on, else there is a chance that you will not get any notification about the error.

See also

- There are more options that can be set for a full overview. I suggest you read the following page:

    https://www.zabbix.com/documentation/2.4/manual/config/items/itemtypes/log_items.

Trigger constructor

Of course, building triggers is nice but it would not be helpful if we had to memorize all possible functions. For this, we can make use of the **trigger** constructor in Zabbix. The constructor will show us a list where we can choose from and easily modify it to our needs.

Getting ready

To be able to do this recipe, you need a Zabbix server with super administrator access such as the standard admin account that came with the installation. We also need a network device that we can monitor in Zabbix.

How to do it...

1. Our first step is to create a simple check. Our simple check will launch a ping command to our host. As host, you can choose any network device that is pingable. If you don't know how to do this, I suggest you go back to *Chapter 4*, *Monitoring with Zabbix* and check out the recipe, *Simple checks*. Just a basic ping check will do. There is no need to add special options to the item.

2. Go to your host. This can be done from the menu **Configuration | Hosts** and click there on **Triggers**.

3. Fill in the **Name** field. example. `Zabbix agent on {HOST.NAME} is unreachable for 5 minutes`. You see in the name {HOST.NAME}, this is a macro that will tell us the hostname when the trigger launches. This will make our life very easy when we get notified later about potential issues.

4. Now instead of typing in the expression, we click on the **Add** button on the right side of the **Expression** box.

Condition - Google Chrome		
🗋 192.168.10.107/zabbix/popup_trexpr.php		

Trigger expression condition

Item	host2: Agent ping	Select
Function	No data received during period of time T, then N = 1, 0 - otherwise	▼
Last of (T)	5m	Time
N	1	

Insert	Cancel

5. We press the **Select** button and another window will pop up where we can select the correct item from our host or template that we will use to build our trigger on.

Items - Google Chrome		
🗋 192.168.10.107/zabbix/popup.php		

Items   Group aggregated ▼ Host host2 ▼

Name	Key	Type	Type of information	Status
Agent ping	agent.ping	Zabbix agent	Numeric (unsigned)	Enabled
Available memory	vm.memory.size[available]	Zabbix agent	Numeric (unsigned)	Enabled
Check Issue	ssh.run[test]	SSH agent	Text	Not supported
Checksum of /etc/passwd	vfs.file.cksum[/etc/passwd]	Zabbix agent	Numeric (unsigned)	Enabled
Context switches per second	system.cpu.switches	Zabbix agent	Numeric (unsigned)	Enabled
CPU idle time	system.cpu.util[,idle]	Zabbix agent	Numeric (float)	Enabled
CPU interrupt time	system.cpu.util[,interrupt]	Zabbix agent	Numeric (float)	Enabled

6. Once you have select the correct trigger, fill in the **Function**. You will also see a drop down list to choose from.

7. For the **Last of** (**T**) option, we fill in 5m, because we only want to be notified once the machine is unreachable for 5 minutes.

8. And for **N** we place 1, because our ping will return 1 if all is fine and 0 when there is a problem.

9. Now our trigger is ready to use.

How it works

Just like in the previous recipe, we have built the same trigger but we made use of the expression builder that is integrated in Zabbix. This will make building complex triggers easier.

There's more

When you click on the **Expression constructor**, some new boxes will pop up under the **Expression** box. You will see the box **And, Or**, and **Replace**. It is possible now to combine two or more expressions with **And** and **Or** to help you out in more complex situations.

See also

▶ https://www.zabbix.com/documentation/2.4/manual/config/
  triggers/expression.

More advanced triggers

Sometimes triggers in Zabbix are too sensitive and you get notifications all the time because of quick repeated status changes; this is what we call flapping. This could be for example a swap file that is growing and shrinking all the time, making Zabbix send notifications that there is not enough free space left and a few seconds later going back in an OK state because there is enough space again to come back in alarm once again, a few seconds later. Another example of flapping could be the CPU load going over and under the threshold every x number of seconds. Let's see how we can solve this.

Getting ready

For this recipe, we only need a Zabbix server with an agent installed on the Zabbix server or some host and of course access with a super administrator account, like the one that comes standard with the installation.

How to do it ...

1. Let's monitor the free space left for our our MySQL database. Create an item that checks the value of the free space of a MySQL volume in percent or if you prefer another volume on your hard drive.

2. If you don't know how to create items, have a look at *Chapter 4, Monitoring Zabbix*.

3. Next go to **Configuration | Hosts | Triggers** and press the **Create a trigger** button for this item.

4. Add this code in the expression box and adjust the volume for MySQLto your needs:

   ```
   ({TRIGGER.VALUE}=0 &
   {MySQL:vfs.fs.size[/var/lib/mysql,pfree].last(0)}<10)
   |
   ({TRIGGER.VALUE}=1 &
   {MySQL:vfs.fs.size[/var/lib/mysql,pfree].last(0)}<30)
   ```

5. Fill in the **Name** of your trigger and select a **Severity**.

6. Save your trigger and try to add some extra data to your volume to see if it works.

How it works

We made use of a new macro, {trigger.value}. We know that once a trigger is in the problem state, it is 1 and once a trigger is in the OK state it is 0. By making use of the operator OR operator (|) we can tell our trigger to change to a problem state if our volume is less than 10 GB, or to remain into a problem state if the state was already in error and the volume has still less than 30 GB free space left.

Our trigger will come back in the OK state once the free space in our volume is more than 30 GB. This is possible because the macro {TRIGGER.VALUE} always returns the current trigger value. The first line defines when the problem starts. In our case, when there is less than 10 percent free space for the MySQL volume.

The second line defines the condition that keeps our trigger in problem state. In our case, this will be less than 30 percent free space.

There's more...

There are more ways to do smart monitoring, for example, we can make use of the fuzzytime() function to see if there is still contact with our proxy. Example: {Zabbix server:zabbix[proxy,<proxy name>,last access].fuzzytime(300)}=0. This will alarm us if there is no contact for 300 seconds.

We can also do a time shift in Zabbix. This means that we can compare a value from an item with the value from example:

```
yesterday.
server:system.cpu.load.avg(1h) }/{server:system.cpu.load.avg(1h,1d)
}>2
```

This expression for example will check the load for 1h today and verify it with our server with the load from yesterday and give a warning if the load is more than 2 times.

See also

- https://www.zabbix.com/documentation/2.4/manual/config/triggers/expression.

Testing our trigger expressions

We have seen so far that we can build triggers by hand and by selecting triggers from a list. What we have not seen yet is a way to test our triggers before throwing everything in production. In this recipe, we will show you how to test the triggers you have just created.

Getting ready

For this recipe, we will need as always our Zabbix server properly set up with a super administrator account. You should also be familiar with creating items and triggers. In this recipe we will make use again of the ping item that we have created in our recipe, *Creating triggers*.

How to do it ...

1. Go back to the trigger that we have created for our item that was checking the availability of our host by making use of ping.

2. Edit the trigger that we have created in our recipe, *Creating triggers*:

Target	Expression	Error	Action
☑	A {Template App Zabbix Agent:agent.ping.nodata(5m)}=1	☑	Delete
Test			

Close expression constructor

3. Click on **Expression constructor**; you will now see a new box with our expression.

4. At the left bottom of the box there is a small button named **Test**. Click on it and a new window will popup:

	Expression Variable Elements	Result type	Value
Test data	{Template App Zabbix Agent:agent.ping.nodata(5m)}	0 or 1	1 ▾
	Expression	Result	
Result	A {Template App Zabbix Agent:agent.ping.nodata(5m)}=1	TRUE	
	A	TRUE	

5. As you can see we have our trigger expression and behind it a value of 1 or 0 that we can select. In our case, if ping is successful it will return a value of **1** and **0** if our ping fails.

6. So select a value of 1 and 0 and press the **Test** button to check the outcome. If everything was created fine then 1 should return us the status **True** and 0 **False**.

How it works

With the expression constructor, it is easy to build more complex constructions but also to test our expressions. By faking a positive or a negative outcome of the input we can see what the outcome will be for our trigger. Zabbix will show us **True** or **False** to let us know what the output will be. This way, it is possible to test the triggers that we have build before putting them in production without knowing if they will work or not.

There's more...

We have seen in this chapter that the severity can be chosen for each trigger that we build. However, it is possible to rename them and to change the colors per severity. The GUI elements can be configured in **Administration | General | Trigger severities**. Users can also set audio alerts. Remember this was explained in *Chapter 2, Exploring the frontend*.

Working with Templates

6

In this chapter, we will cover the following topics:

- ▶ Creating templates
- ▶ Importing and exporting templates
- ▶ Linking templates
- ▶ Nesting templates
- ▶ Macros in templates

Introduction

So far in previous chapters, we have seen how to add hosts, create items, and add triggers to those items. Now imagine you have 10 servers with PostgreSQL and you want to monitor them. What will you do? You possibly will create items for each host to gather data and add triggers for each item. We then could copy all items and triggers 10 times to all other hosts. But what if you need to make changes? You will change it again on all hosts individually? What if we have to do this on 100 hosts, program something with the API? To make our life easier, we have templates in Zabbix. With templates we only have to create 1 item and 1 trigger. We can then link this template to all our hosts and reuse all our work over and over.

Creating templates

In this recipe, we will show you how you can create templates in Zabbix. It's always advised to use templates as much as possible.

Getting ready

For this recipe, we need a Zabbix server and access to the server with a Zabbix administrator or super administrator account.

How to do it ...

1. From the menu, go to **Configuration | Templates**.
2. Click on the **Template** button on the upper right corner.
3. In the field **Template name**, you can write the name of your template, example. PostgreSQL template.
4. In the box **Visible name**, you can add a name that will be visible in Zabbix in case that the name of your template is too long or too cryptic for some reason.
5. In **Groups**, we will choose the group to which our template belongs. Here we select `Templates` as group.
6. In the **Description** box we can write a note. This can be handy for later if the name of your template is not informative enough to know what you monitor.
7. Next we click **Add** to save our templates.

8. From the **Configuration | Templates** page, we can now see our template in the list of templates.

9. As you can see each template has the option to add applications, items, triggers, graphs, screens, and so on, just like we had on our hosts.

How it works

Templates are just a collection of items, triggers, applications, and so on, that we can reuse. Instead of creating each item or trigger and so on on every host, we just create a template. Then we make everything in our template and link it to a bunch of hosts so that we can reuse our work.

There's more...

Templates are often used to link servers with the same service or application such as PostgreSQL, Apache, Zabbix agent, Red Hat, Ubuntu, proxies, and so.

Since Zabbix 2.2, web scenarios were added to the template. When you edit a already saved template, you will see some extra buttons at the end of the page. The **Update** button will, of course, update any changes made. The **Clone** button will duplicate your template into a new template and copy all entities like triggers, items, and so on inherited from linked templates. The **Full clone** will do the same as the **Clone** button but also copy directly attached items, triggers, and so on, from the template to the new template. **Delete** will obviously delete your template but all items will remain with the host while **Delete and clear** will remove all items from the linked hosts.

 You cannot link a template to a host, if the template has items that are already on the host as each item on a host has to be unique.

See also

▸ https://www.zabbix.com/documentation/2.4/manual/config/templates.

Importing and exporting templates

When we have templates made in Zabbix, it makes sense to back them up in case we want to use them later or to share them with, for instance, the community. In this recipe, we will show you how to import and export templates in Zabbix.

Getting ready

What do we need for this recipe? We need our Zabbix server properly set up. For this setup to work we also need an administrator or super administrator account.

How to do it...

1. To export our template, we have to go in our menu to **Configuration | Templates**.

2. Next, we select the template that we would like to export and select **Export selected** from the dropdown box.

3. Click on **Go**, now Zabbix will export the template in XML format to our disk.

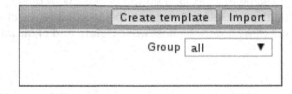

When we want to import templates we have to follow more or less the same steps:

1. Our first step is to go to **Configuration | Templates**.

2. On the upper right corner, click **Import**.

3. We now see a box where we can select the file that we want to import.

4. Make a selection of the possible options. There is a column to update missing data in case our template was already installed on our system and we wanted to update it with new features. We also have a column for new templates in case we don't want to install everything from our template. When importing hosts / templates using the **Delete missing** option, host / template macros not present in the imported XML file will be deleted too.

	Update existing	Create new	Delete missing
Import file Choose file No file chosen			
Rules			
Groups		✔	
Hosts	☐	☐	
Templates	✔	✔	
Template screens	✔	✔	☐
Template linkage		✔	
Applications		✔	☐
Items	✔	✔	☐
Discovery rules	✔	✔	☐
Triggers	✔	✔	☐
Graphs	✔	✔	☐
Screens	☐	☐	
Maps	☐	☐	
Images	☐	☐	

Import   Cancel

How it works

Importing and exporting templates is very straightforward. When we want to export a template, we only have to select what template we want to export and click on the Export button. Zabbix will export the template in a file that we can download. The format of this file is XML.

When we want to import templates we have some more options. When importing templates we have the options to update existing templates or to import them and make a choice of what we would like to import.

There's more...

Besides templates, we can export and import also hosts, host groups, network maps, images, and screens. Images are exported in a Base64 format.

Import and exporting templates can be useful in case you want to back up your templates. It can also be useful if you have a development and a production environment. This way you could develop and test everything first on the development machine, export templates and import them on the production environment.

Another way is to share them with the community (I highly recommend you to do this).

See also

▸ https://www.zabbix.com/documentation/2.4/manual/xml_export_
  import?s[]=import&s[]=templates

▸ http://en.wikipedia.org/wiki/Base64

▸ http://zabbix.org/wiki/Zabbix_Templates

Linking templates

Having templates is great, but you probably want to link it to a host as well, else we would not have much use of our templates. In this recipe, we will show you how to link those templates to your hosts.

Getting ready

For this recipe, we need a Zabbix server and access to the server with a Zabbix administrator or super administrator account. We also need a fresh host.

How to do it ...

1. Go back to the menu **Configuration | Templates**.
2. Select a template from the list, example. `Template App Zabbix Agent`. This can be done by clicking on its template name.
3. From the box **Other | group**, select the fresh host that you would like to link with this template and press the **<<** button to move it to the box **Hosts / Templates**.

CONFIGURATION OF TEMPLATES

« Template list   **Template:** Template App Zabbix Agent   Applications (1)   Items (3)   Triggers (3)   Graphs (0)   Screens (0)   Discovery rules (0)   Web scenarios (0)

| Template | Linked templates | Macros |

Template name   Template App Zabbix Agent

Visible name

Groups   In groups

Templates

Other groups

Discovered hosts
Hypervisors
Linux servers
Virtual machines
Zabbix servers

New group

Hosts / templates   In

Template OS AIX
Template OS FreeBSD
Template OS HP-UX
Template OS Linux
Template OS Mac OS X
Template OS OpenBSD
Template OS Solaris
Template OS Windows

Other | group   Linux servers

JMX Host

4. Press the **Update** button at the bottom of the page.

> There are probably already a few names in the box **Hosts / Templates**. Don't worry, those are already hosts or other templates that are linked to this template.

How it works

We need to link our templates to hosts after we have created them. This way it is possible to link our template to multiple hosts.

It is also possible to link templates from the host itself. This can be done by clicking on the host from the menu **Configuration | Hosts**. You then select the **Templates** tab and select a new template from the list or type the name in the **Link new templates** box. Don't forget to click **Add** afterwards to add your template to the host.

See also

> ▶ https://www.zabbix.com/documentation/2.4/manual/config/templates/linking.

Nesting templates

It is also possible in Zabbix to link templates with each other. This may sound weird and unnecessary at first but it's definitely a great feature. Imagine you have a web server with Apache, MySQL, and PHP. You could create 1 big template to monitor all items or you could create 3 templates. One for Apache, one for MySQL, and another one for PHP. But what if you have another web server that you would like to monitor? Do you add those three templates again to that host? What you could do in this case is create a new template `Webserver` and link it with the three templates we mentioned earlier. In this case, we only have to link 1 template `Webserver` to our webserver and we can still use the template Apache or MySQL in case we only want to monitor Apache or MySQL on another server.

Getting ready

To be able to do this recipe, you need a Zabbix server properly set up with an admin account or super administrator account setup.

How to do it...

1. From the menu go, to **Configuration | Templates**.

2. Click **Create New Template**.

3. Fill in the **Template name**, example. `Webserver Template`.

4. Add it in the group templates.

5. Select **Linked templates** from the tab on top.

6. In the box **Link new templates**, click the **Select** button.

7. From the popup window select `Template App HTTP Service` and `Template App Mysql`.

8. Click the **Select** button at the bottom.

Template	Linked templates	Macros		
	Linked templates	**Name** **Action**		
		No templates linked.		
	Link new templates	Template App HTTP Service ✕ Template App MySQL ✕	Select	
		Add		
		Update	Clone	Full clone	Delete	Delete and clear	Cancel

9. Back in the menu **Linked templates**, you now see the two templates we have selected, we still have to click **Add**.

10. And finally click **Update**.

How it works

In the template menu we just create a new template. This template we link to two or more templates so that our new template will inherit all of the items of the linked templates. Our new template will then be linked to our host. This way we don't have to link two templates to our host but only one. Later it is possible to link more templates to the new template we have made.

 In the **Link new templates box**, it is possible to type the name of the template if you know the name or part of the name, and then select it from a popup window.

There's more...

When we go back to the menu Configuration | Templates, we will see our template web server and in the column Linked templates we will see the names of the templates linked to our new template.

| Webserver Template | Applications (2) Items (15) Triggers (2) Graphs (2) Screens (0) Discovery (0) Web (0) Template App HTTP Service, Template App MySQL |

See also

▶ https://www.zabbix.com/documentation/2.4/manual/config/templates/nesting

Macros in templates

If you have a lot of servers then you probably want to have your templates a bit more dynamic. There are probably also some cases where a certain value in your template is not fit for just one server in your park. For this, we can make use of macros in our templates.

Getting ready

For this recipe to work, we need a Zabbix server and a Zabbix host. We also need to make sure that we have a SSH session active on port 22 on our host as we will monitor the SSH service on our host. For this, we will make use of macros. We also need to make use of the super administrator account in Zabbix.

How to do it ...

1. First thing that we need to do is to go to **Administration | general | Macros** in our Zabbix menu. (Macros can be selected from the dropdown menu on the right).

2. In the **Macros** menu, add a new macro {$SSH_PORT} and give it the value 422 or something other than 22. It must be a port that is not in use by SSH.

Macros				
	Macro		Value	
	{$SNMP_COMMUNITY}	→	public	Remove
	{$SSH_PORT}	→	422	Remove
	Add			
	Update			

Zabbix 2.4.0 Copyright 2001-2014 by Zabbix SIA

3. Now go to **Configuration | Template** and create a new template with the name Template SSH port.

4. Link the template to your client and save it.

5. Next go to the **Items** in your template and create a new item.

6. Add a **Name** `Check SSH port $3`.

7. Select **Type** as `Simple check`.

8. Add the following **Key**: `net.tcp.service[ssh,,{$SSH_PORT}]`

9. The **Type of information** should be `Numeric`.

10. **Data type** should be `Decimal`.

11. Give in **New application**, an application name example. `ssh check`.

12. Save your item.

Item	
Name	Check SSH Port $3
Type	Simple check ▼
Key	net.tcp.service[ssh.,{$SSH_PORT}] Select
User name	
Password	
Type of information	Numeric (unsigned) ▼
Data type	Decimal ▼
Units	
Use custom multiplier	☐ 1
Update interval (in sec)	30
Flexible intervals	Interval Period Action
	No flexible intervals defined.
New flexible interval	Interval (in sec) 50 Period 1-7,00:00-24:00 Add
History storage period (in days)	90
Trend storage period (in days)	365
Store value	As is ▼
Show value	As is ▼ show value mappings
New application	
Applications	-None- ssh check

13. Next we go to our host again from the menu **Configuration | Hosts**.

14. We then go to the tab **Macros** in our host.

CONFIGURATION OF HOSTS	
« Host list **Host:** client Enabled Applications (1) Items (1) Triggers (0) Graphs (0) Discovery rules (0) Web scenarios (0)	
Host Templates IPMI **Macros** Host inventory	
Macro	Value
{$SSH_PORT}	→ 22 Remove
Add	

Update   Clone   Full clone   Delete   Cancel

15. Here we add the macro {$SSH_PORT} with value 22.

16. We now save our work.

17. Next when we go to **Monitoring | Latest data**, we will see that on our host for the SSH port the status is **1**. This means that our service is up.

How it works

In the **Administration** panel under **General | Macros**, we can define global macros. Those global macros can be used in our templates. So by defining {$SSH_PORT} macro in our item to monitor the SSH port, we were telling our template to look to the global macro. This means that our template would always check, in this case, port 422. Because we defined a new macro on our host with the value 22, that specific macro was over written for only this particular host. So in our case the template would always look for a service on port 422, but only for our host it would look for a service on port 22.

See also

► https://www.zabbix.com/documentation/2.4/manual/config/macros/usermacros

► A complete list of supported macros can be found here:

   https://www.zabbix.com/documentation/2.4/manual/appendix/macros/supported_by_location#additional_support_for_user_macros

7
Data Visualization and Reporting in Zabbix

In this chapter, we will cover the following topics:

- Creating graphs
- Creating screens
- Creating slideshows
- Building maps in Zabbix
- Creating reports
- Generating SLA reports

Introduction

In the previous chapters, we have seen how to create items and build thresholds for those items. Our next step is to visualize this data. So in this chapter, we will show you how to visualize your data in Zabbix by building graphs, screens, maps, and put it all together in a slideshow. When all this is finished, we will generate some reports from our data and build some graphs based on SLA's that we set in Zabbix.

Creating graphs

In this recipe, we will show you how to build some nice looking graphs from the data that we have gathered from our items.

Getting ready

For this recipe, we need a Zabbix installation and an agent installed on the Zabbix server or another host that we can use. We also need admin rights in Zabbix to be able to create our graph.

How to do it...

1. First we need an item. For this we will monitor our CPU load as it always gives a nice graph. Add an item `system.cpu.load[percpu,avg1]`. If you don't know how to do this, have look at *Chapter 4, Passive agents* or *Active agents*.

2. Next go to **Configuration | Hosts**, then go to **Configuration | Template** if you would like to create it in a template.

3. Click on the **Graphs** link after your host and click **Create graph** in the upper right corner.

4. In the **Name** box we add a name for our graph, example: `CPU load`.

5. We can set the **Width** and the **Height** of our graph.

6. Next we select the **Graph type**. This can be `Normal`, `Stacked`, `Pie`, or `Exploded`. `Normal` is with lines, `Stacked` is layers above each other and `Pie` / `Exploded` is a representation in a pie form. `Exploded` is almost exactly the same except that it shows the individual segments of the pie in an exploded view.

7. The **Show legend** will display the graphs legend if marked.

8. The **Show working time** box will show the working hours in our graph. (Remember those can be set under **Administration | General | Working time**).

9. **Percentile line** (**left | right**) will set the percent for the graph left or right. This only works for normal graphs.

10. **Y axis** (**Min | Max**) **value** will be the maximum or minimum value for our Y axis. This can be changed in `Calculated`, `Fixed`, or `Item`. When choosing `Calculated` those will be calculated by Zabbix. `Fixed` will set a fixed min or max value. This can't be done for `pie` and `exploded pie`. When we choose X, it will be the last value of the selected item.

11. When we select `pie` or `exploded pie`, we also have the option **3D view** which will create a 3D view of our pie.

12. Next we click on **Add** in the **Items** box and we add our item. This we can select from the list of items that will pop up.

13. Next select the **Function** here; we can choose `avg`, `max`, and `min`. This will show us the average minimum or maximum values.

14. **Y axis side** can be switched from `Left` to `Right`.

15. And in the **Colour** box, we can choose another color by adding the correct RGB color in hex notation or by clicking on the color box and choosing a new color from the list of colors.

16. When this is all done we can save our graph.

How it works

For every item in Zabbix, we can create a graph. For this, we should select the item that the graph should check. We can select more then one item from the item box. Another great feature is that we can mix different items in one graph, example. CPU load, Memory usage, Disk I/O, and so on. This way we could, for instance, see the impact of memory usage on other parts of our system.

There's more...

We can make use of macros in map names but have to do it a bit differently. We have to add it with this syntax: `{host:key.function(param)}`. In our case, it would look like this, CPU load `{{HOST.HOST}:system.cpu.load[percpu,avg1].last(0)}`. This example would return a header such as: CPU load 0.5.

Also Zabbix supports some graphs out of the box. That means if you add a Zabbix template to your host, it will probably already contain some graphs.

Since Zabbix 2.4, there is support for ad hoc graphs on several items. When you go to monitor latest data you will have the option **Graph** behind most of the items. By clicking on this link, you will see a graph built by Zabbix for this item.

Last check	Last value	Change	
2014-11-01 11:30:18	62 sps	+3 sps	Graph
2014-11-01 11:30:19	98.09 %	-0.67 %	Graph
2014-11-01 11:30:20	0.03 %	-0.01 %	Graph
2014-11-01 11:30:21	0.72 %	+0.28 %	Graph
2014-11-01 11:30:22	0 %	-	Graph

See also

> ► A full list of macros that can be used can be found here:
>
>   `https://www.zabbix.com/documentation/2.4/manual/appendix/`
>   `macros/supported_by_location`

Creating screens

Sometimes we want to see different kinds of data from our servers at the same time. Problem is that this always doesn't make sense. Sometimes we want to see CPU load, memory, network traffic, even from different servers, but we don't want to see it in one graph all together. For this, we have screens in Zabbix. Screens in Zabbix are a quick way to display different kinds of information in something that looks like a table on your screen. In screens, we can display graphs, maps, other screens, and much more. Screens can be useful for service centers as we put all data for them in one or more screens so that there is an easy overview; for example, data from all webservers or load balancers in one screen.

Getting ready

For this recipe, we obviously need our Zabbix server and a Zabbix account with administrator rights. We also need an agent installed on our Zabbix server and the template `Template App Zabbix Server` linked to our host.

How to do it...

1. From the menu, go to **Configuration | Screens**.
2. Click on the **Create screen** button in the upper right corner. We will ignore the screen that is already there. Later you can edit the standard screen or remove it if you like.

3. First thing to do is add a **Name** for our **Screen**, example. `Zabbix server`.

4. Next we add the number of **Columns** that we want to have in our screen.

5. The last thing we have to change is the number of **Rows** in our screen that we want to have.

6. Click **Add** to create our screen.

CONFIGURATION OF SCREENS

Screen

Name	Zabbix server
Columns	4
Rows	2

Add   Cancel

Zabbix 2.4.0 Copyright 2001-2014 by Zabbix SIA

7. You will see now under **Configuration | Screens** that we have created a screen with our name. Click on the **Name** of the screen you have created, `Zabbix server`.

8. You will now see a table with exactly the same amount of columns and rows as you have entered before. In each field, you will also see the name **Change**. Click on **Change** in a field to change the content of this field.

Screen cell configuration

Resource	Graph
Graph name	select
Width	500
Height	100
Horizontal align	Left Center Right
Vertical align	Top Middle Bottom
Column span	1
Row span	1
Dynamic item	

Add   Cancel

Change

Change   Change

9. Select the kind of **Resource** that you want to see visualized. For this recipe, we will select a `Graph`.

10. Add a **Graph name**; we can select an item from the list that is available for our server by pressing the **Select** button, example. `Zabbix server performance`.

11. Adjust the **Width** and **Height** for the graph if you like.

12. Let Zabbix know if we have to align it horizontally or vertically to the `Left`, `Right`, `Top`, `Bottom`, `Middle`, or `Center`.

13. Next we have **Column span** and **Row span**. This works exactly like in HTML. We can tell how many columns or rows our item has to use.

14. Next we have an interesting option, **Dynamic item**. If we select it, we will see when we go to our screen that our screen item is available for all hosts.

15. Lets add some other items to our screen, for example, a clock or something else that you would like to see.

16. Now lets have a look at it by going to the menu **Monitoring | Screens**.

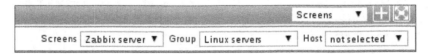

17. If you have selected **Dynamic item**, you will see in the top right corner a box as shown the picture below, where you can select another server or group for this item.

How it works

Screens are a just a collection of all kinds of information brought together in a table-like view. First thing we have to do when creating screens is think how many columns and rows we would like to have. This is not fixed, we can still change it later. When we want to add certain items to our fields, we can choose from the following list:

▶ **Action log**: A history of recent actions

▶ **Clock**: Digital or analog clock displaying current server or local time

▶ **Data overview**: Shows latest data for a group of hosts

- **Graph**: A single custom graph that you created before on a host or a template
- **Graph prototype**: A custom graph from low-level discovery rule (new since Zabbix 2.4
- **History of events**: Shows the latest events
- **Host group issues**: Status of triggers filtered by the hostgroup (includes triggers without events, since Zabbix 2.2)
- **Host issues**: Status of triggers filtered by the host (includes triggers without events, since Zabbix 2.2)
- **Hosts info**: High-level host related information
- **Map**: Displays a previously created single map
- **Plain text**: Plain text data measured from an item
- **Screen**: Screen (You can display a screen in another screen)
- **Server info**: Displays server information like number of monitored hosts and item.
- **Simple graph**: Single simple graph
- **Simple graph prototype**: Simple graph based on item generated by low-level discovery (available since Zabbix 2.4)
- **System status**: Displays system status (similar to the dashboard)
- **Triggers info**: High-level trigger related information
- **Triggers overview**: Displays a table with the status of all triggers of a host group-includes content from an external resource

There's more...

Triggers will not be displayed in the legend if the height from a graph is set less then 120 pixels. In the screen, you have probably noticed + and - symbols on the sides of each table. When you click on the + symbol above the table, a new column will be added. Clicking on the – symbol will remove a column. Similarly, when we click on the left side of the table on the + symbol, a new row will be added. Clicking on the – symbol will remove a row.

See also

- https://www.zabbix.com/documentation/2.4/manual/config/visualisation/screens

Creating slideshows

Besides the possibility to integrate multiple small screens in a big screen, it is also possible to combine multiple screens into a so-called slideshow. In a slideshow, the screens are shown one after another.

Getting ready

For this recipe, we need a Zabbix server properly configured and access to a Zabbix admin account. We also need to have 2 or more screens configured. If you don't know how to configure screens, then have a look at *Chapter 7, Creating screens*.

How to do it...

1. From the menu go to **Configuration | Slideshows**.
2. In the upper right corner, click on **Create slideshow**.
3. In the **Name** field we add a name for our slideshow.
4. **Default delay (in seconds)**, here we add the delay between each screen.
5. In the **Slides** field, we press the **Add** button and select from the popup box the screens that we want to add to our slides.
6. You will see a **Delay** box after each **Screen**. Here we can choose a delay different than the `default` delay we have chosen for each slide.
7. When you are ready, click the **Add** button to save our slideshow.

8. To watch our slideshow, go to **Monitoring | Screens** and select `Slide shows` from the dropdown box on the upper right corner.

| | Slide shows ▼ | ➕ | 🔳 | ✛ |
| Slide show | My slideshow ▼ | Group | all ▼ | Host | not selected ▼ |

9. On the right side of slideshow we see three icons. The first one is a plus icon; this is to add our slideshow to our favorites. The second icons will show us a list of multipliers that we can use to manipulate the time between the slides. The third icon will show the slideshow in fullscreen mode.

How it works

Slideshows in Zabbix are built from screens. So the first thing we have to do is create screens in Zabbix that we like. We can then create a slideshow from it by adding screens to the slideshow. It is possible to create multiple slideshows.

There's more...

In slideshows the minimum time between 2 screens is 5 seconds. Even if you put 2 or 4 seconds the minimum delay will be 5. If you try to fool Zabbix by creating a delay of 5 and using the multiplier of 0.5, then the delay between 2 screens will still be 5 seconds.

See also

▸ https://www.zabbix.com/documentation/2.4/manual/config/visualisation/slides

Building maps in Zabbix

Maps in Zabbix are a visual representation of your infrastructure. In maps, it is possible to see where the problems are in a visual way. Maps are a kind of interactive network diagrams where we connect individual elements with lines that can show us when a host is unreachable.

Getting ready

For this Zabbix recipe to work, we need a Zabbix server and a host with on server and host a Zabbix client installed. We also need to have the Zabbix server templates attached to the server and the Linux OS templates attached to both hosts. We obviously also need a Zabbix account with super administration rights.

How to do it...

1. Go in the Zabbix menu to **Configuration | Maps**.

2. We will see that there is already a map available. We can edit this one but in this case we will just start with a new map; so click the **Create map** button.

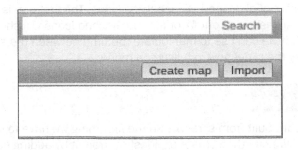

3. When we create a new map, we get a window where we have to give a name to our map. We can fill in the **Name** here of our network.

4. The **Width** and **Height** probably explain themselves. Those are the dimensions of our map later on the screen of our computer (or TV on the wall).

5. The option **Background image** will allow us to select an image as background for our map. It's probably empty and the only way to add a background image in the list is by adding one in the menu under **Administration | General | Images**.

6. One of the options available to automate things is the **Automatic icon mapping**. This can be configured under **Administration | General | Icon mapping**. We can automatically link an icon to a server based on the inventory that we have populated and a `regexp`.

7. The option **Icon highlight** will highlight the icons on our map when triggers go into alarm. Items with an active trigger will receive a round background, in the same color as the highest severity trigger. A thick green line will be displayed around the circle once all problems are acknowledged. Items that are `disabled` or `in maintenance` status will get a square background in gray and orange respectively.

8. The option **Mark elements on trigger status change** will help us show recent changes of a trigger status. Recent problems will be highlighted with markers (red triangles) on the three sides of the element icon that are free of the label. Those markers are displayed for 30 minutes.

9. The **Expand single problem** will show the name of the problem on the map if an element (host, host group, or another map) has a single problem. This option controls whether the problem name (trigger) is displayed or the problem count.

10. When selecting **Advanced labels**, new dropdown boxes will show up and you will be able to define separate label types for separate element types.

11. The **Icon label type** will only be visible; if not, select the **Advanced labels** box which will help us set the label for all types.

12. The **Icon label location** will define the location of our label. This can be at the Bottom, Left, Right, or Top of our icon.

13. The option **Problem display** will give us the option to select All, Separated, and Unacknowledged only. All will show a complete problem count. Separated will display unacknowledged problems separated. Unacknowledged only will only show the unacknowledged problem count.

14. **Minimum trigger severity** is new since Zabbix 2.2 and will only show triggers on the map that fit the minimum selected trigger severity.

15. **URLs** can be used for each kind of element with a label. They will be displayed as a link when a user clicks on the element in the monitoring section. We can make use of macros in the **URL** section, for example, {MAP.ID}, {HOSTGROUP.ID}, {HOST.ID}, {TRIGGER.ID}.

16. Press the **Add** button when you have selected the options you like.

17. Now click on the name of your map from the list of maps.

18. Make sure that **Expand macros** is on, else we cannot make use of macros in our map.

19. Press the + button next to **Icon** and select for **Type** Host.

20. Add a **Label**; this can be just a name or a macro such as {HOST.HOST} to generate the hostname automatic. (Check the list of macros to see what other macros you can use).

21. Add our Zabbix server on the map just like we did with our agent.

   ❑ Next press the *Ctrl* button on your keyboard and select both the agent and Zabbix server, and then press the + button next to **Link** to create a link between agent and server.

22. At the bottom, we see **Links between the selected elements**; here we click on **Edit**. We will see a new box where we can fill in a new label, and so on.

23. In the **Label** box we add `Out: {Zabbix server:net.if.out[eth0].last(0)}`, where Zabbix server should be replaced with the hostname of your Zabbix server.

24. The **Type(OK)** box can be used to change the type of line we want to see in an OK status.

25. The **Colour(OK)** box lets us select the color of the line in OK status.

26. In the box **Link indicators**, we can add a trigger, for example. the trigger that checks with a ping if our host is available. If the trigger goes into alarm, we could change the line in a broken red line to show that we have issues with our connection.

27. Click **Apply** and close the box and then click **Update** in the map menu. This is important! Else you will lose all modifications made to the map.

28. Now go from the Zabbix menu to **Monitoring | Maps** and select from the dropdown box **Maps** on the right the correct map.

How it works

In Zabbix we can build maps to visualize our environment. We can add backgrounds like the building layout or a world map to visualize the location of our infrastructure. To make our maps more dynamic we can make use of macros. With those macros we can show information that we have gathered from our servers with items. To make things even more dynamic, we can also make use of triggers in our maps to mark on our map when a status is changed, example. when a line goes down or CPU load is too high.

In the link **Label**, we had to specify our hostname instead of using the macro `{HOST.HOST}`. This is because we are linked to two servers and Zabbix will be confused if both servers have the item `net.if.out[eth0]`. So in this case, we have to tell Zabbix from which server we want the data.

There's more...

To align icons on the map, it is possible to work with a grid. Normally, there is a grid visible that we can deactivate in the map menu by selecting **Grid** show on/off. The size of the grid can be changed and we can press the **Align icons** button to align our icons on the grid. When you have a lot of servers in many places, it can make sense to create a map for each location.

It is possible to link maps with maps. Zabbix will show you on the main map when there is an issue in one of the buildings. From the main map, you can then click and go to the map where the issue is.

 If you have a lot of servers on your map all connected with each other by lines, it can make sense to use invisible lines and only show lines in red to mark them as problematic.

See also

▶ https://www.zabbix.com/documentation/2.4/manual/config/visualisation/maps/map

▶ Check the list of supported macros to have an idea what macros can be used or not in maps:

https://www.zabbix.com/documentation/2.4/manual/appendix/macros/supported_by_location

Creating reports

In this recipe, we will show you how to create reports in Zabbix. Zabbix provides us with some predefined reports, but we can also create our own reports.

Getting ready

For this, we need a Zabbix setup properly configured with the Zabbix super administration account.

How to do it...

1. The first step is quite easy; go to the Zabbix menu and **Select Reports | Status of Zabbix**. You will see the status overview of the system.

2. Another report is our availability report; this can be found under **Reports | Availability report**. We can filter in the top right corner by **Host** or by **Trigger** template from the box **Mode**. Press the **Show filter** button on top to fine tune the selection by host, host group, and period.

3. At the end of the page, there is a column **Graph** where we can click on the link **Show** after each host. This will show us a graph in green and red with the status of our item.

4. Yet another report is the **Triggers top 100**. This can be found under **Reports | Triggers top 100**. This report will show us a list of triggers whose status is changed the most during a certain period and we can choose the same from the upper right box.

Host	Trigger	Severity	Number of status changes
Zabbix server	Zabbix server has just been restarted	Information	2
client	/etc/passwd has been changed on client	Warning	1
Zabbix server	/etc/passwd has been changed on Zabbix server	Warning	1
client	client has just been restarted	Information	1
client	Configured max number of opened files is too low on client	Information	1

5. Our last report is the **Bar reports**. This can be found under **Reports | Bar reports**.

6. In the upper right corner, we have a dropdown box where we can select three different options. The first bar report `Distribution of values for multiple periods` offers a possibility to simply compare item values side by side.

7. The second bar report `Distribution of values for multiple items` offers a possibility to compare the values of one or several items in custom periods.

8. The `Compare values for multiple periods` bar report offers a possibility to compare the values of one item for different hosts / predefined intervals (`Hourly` / `Daily` / `Weekly` / `Monthly` / `Yearly`).

9. In this report, we can select an item and then select groups and hosts.

10. We can filter that data by a certain **Period** of time.

11. The **Scale** option does the same as the above but in a more fine-tuned way such as on a `Weekly`, `Hourly`, or `Daily` basis.

12. The **Average by** option will show in the bars the average value on a `Weekly`, `Monthly`, `Yearly`, and so on basis.

13. **Palette** will give you the ability to change the colors and the intensity.

Title	Report 3
X label	
Y label	
Legend	☐

	Selected groups		Other groups
Groups	Linux servers	« »	Zabbix servers

	Selected hosts		Other hosts | Group All ▼
Hosts	client Zabbix server	« »	

Period	From	2014 - 11 - 10 00 : 00
	Till	2014 - 11 - 11 00 : 00
Scale	Daily ▼	
Average by	Daily ▼	
Item	CPU iowait time	Select
Palette	Palette #2 ▼ Darken ▼	

Show Reset

One of the limitations in Zabbix is that when we create reports, they will be created on the fly but there is no option to save them. In big setups creating reports on the fly can be database-intensive. The **STATUS OF ZABBIX** is exactly the same as the status on the front page of Zabbix that is only available for the super administrator accounts.

How it works

In the reports menu, we have a few options in Zabbix. First, we have the **STATUS OF ZABBIX** that shows us exactly what the super administrator sees on the front page of Zabbix. Next we have the **Availability report** and the **Triggers top 100** report where we make use of `host` or `hostgroup` and time to see some information from our items.

The option **Bar reports** gives us a more flexible way to visualize our data and gives us also the possibility to scale our data based on certain periods.

See also

▶ `https://www.zabbix.com/documentation/2.4/manual/web_interface/` `frontend_sections/reports`.

Generating SLA reports

Most of the times, managers are not interested in how much disk capacity we have or how many CPUs we have in our servers. They are more interested in whether or not we are able to deliver our services. So in Zabbix SLA reporting is called IT services.

Getting ready

For IT services to work, we only need a properly configured Zabbix server with administration rights. It is also good to have the agent installed on your server to have it linked with the agent template.

How to do it...

1. From the Zabbix menu, go to **Configuration | IT services**.
2. You will see the **root** service; click on it and select **Add a child**.
3. In the **Name** field we add `Zabbix Server SLA` or another name that makes sense.
4. In the **Status calculation** algorithm we have three options to choose from:
    - `Do not calculate`: This option will not calculate the service status.
    - `Problem, if at least one child has a problem`: This option will change to problem status, if at least one child service has a problem.
    - `Problem, if all children have problems`: This will change the status to problem status, if all child services are having problems.

5. In the **Dependencies** tab, we can select what other services this service depends on.

6. In the **Time** tab, we can add time-specific options to select when we have to calculate our IT services.

7. Next, we save our service and we arrive back on the page with the **root** service and under the root our `Zabbix Server SLA` service that we just made.

8. Click on `Zabbix Server SLA` and add a new service just like we did with root in step 2.

9. Add a **Name**, example. `Disk I/O overload`.

10. In **Calculate SLA, acceptable SLA (in %)**, we add a number for our SLA, example. `95.0000`.

Monitoring	Inventory	Reports	Configuration	Administration

Host groups	Templates	Hosts	Maintenance	Actions	Screens	Slide shows	Maps	Discovery	IT services

History: Configuration of IT services » IT services » Latest events » IT services » Configuration of IT services

CONFIGURATION OF IT SERVICES

Service	Dependencies	Time

Name	Disk I/O overload
Parent service	Zabbix Server SLA Change
Status calculation algorithm	Problem, if at least one child has a problem ▼
Calculate SLA, acceptable SLA (in %)	☑ 95.0000
Trigger	Zabbix server: Disk I/O is overloaded on Zabbix server Select
Sort order (0->999)	0

Update   Delete   Cancel

Zabbix 2.4.0 Copyright 2001-2014 by Zabbix SIA

11. All other options can stay and we can click **Add** to save.

12. Now when you go to **Monitoring | IT services**, you will see the SLA service calculated for our disk I/O.

13. When you click on the **Problem time** bar, you will get a bar overview from the whole year.

How it works

IT services are calculated based on our items that we have created. Under the **root**, we had created a service, **Zabbix Server SLA**. Normally you would create there a service per server or per service such as Apache, DNS, and so on.

Then you would, like we did, add all items related to that kind of service. Zabbix will then calculate the SLA per item and show you the total SLA per service.

There's more...

It's good to keep in mind that IT services are calculated from the moment we create them.

See also

▸   https://www.zabbix.com/documentation/2.4/manual/it_services.

8

Monitoring VMware and Proxies

In this chapter, we will cover the following topics:

- ▸ Configuring Zabbix for VMware
- ▸ Monitoring VMware
- ▸ Installing a proxy
- ▸ Setting up an active proxy
- ▸ Setting up a passive proxy
- ▸ Monitoring hosts through a proxy
- ▸ Monitoring the proxy

Introduction

In bigger companies, monitoring will involve virtual machines, machines in DMZ and machines in other locations including other parts of the world.

To help you out with these problems, this chapter will teach you to set up VMware monitoring in Zabbix and also explain you how to set up proxies and use them.

Configuring Zabbix for VMware

When we talk about virtualization, there are many solutions in the market these days. The biggest player is still VMware, and Zabbix made it much easier for us to monitor our VMware infrastructure. In this recipe, we will show you how to set up VMware monitoring in Zabbix.

Getting ready

For this recipe to work, we need of course, a Zabbix server with the necessary admin rights and of course a VMware server that we can monitor. VMware monitoring is available since Zabbix 2.2. The minimum required version of VMware vCenter or vSphere is 4.1.

How to do it...

If you compile Zabbix, then make sure that you compile it with the `--with-libxml2` and `--with-libcurl` options, else VMware monitoring will not work.

1. Since we make use of the packages, the only thing we have to do first is to enable the following options in the `zabbix_server.conf` file:

   - `StartVMwareCollectors = 1`
   - `VMwareCacheSize = 8M`
   - `VMwareFrequency = 60`

2. Make sure you restart the Zabbix server after changes have been made to the `zabbix_server.conf` file.

3. Next, we create a new host for our vCenter in Zabbix under **Configuration | Hosts**, just like we would with any other server.

4. When our host is added, we have to link it to the correct template. Zabbix provides for this with a pre-made template named `Template Virt VMware`:

5. Next we have to add some credentials. Zabbix needs a VMware account that has access to the API. Under **Configuration | Hosts**, there is a tab **Macros** where we have to create 3 macros. First is {$PASSWORD}, we also need to add {$USERNAME} and {$URL}.

The username and password are obvious. For the {$URL} field, we need to add the URL to the vCenter API; this should be `https://MyVcenter/sdk` where `MyVcenter` is the DNS name or even better the IP to your vCenter.

How it works...

Zabbix comes with some ready-made templates to monitor our VMware server. The only thing we need to do is provide Zabbix with the needed credentials such as the username, password, and the proper link to the SDK from our VMware server. It would be best if the account that we use here is an account that is only available for Zabbix as the credentials are easy to read by anyone with Zabbix administration rights.

There's more...

If the user is in a Windows domain, you need to define the macro {$USERNAME} such as this: `MYDomain\SomeUser`.

See also

▶ `https://www.zabbix.com/documentation/2.4/manual/vm_monitoring`

▶ `https://www.zabbix.com/documentation/2.4/manual/vm_monitoring/discovery_fields`

Monitoring VMware

After you have configured VMware in Zabbix, you would obviously like to know how to monitor your infrastructure. Zabbix made this quite easy by providing standard templates and low-level discovery. If you would like to know more about low-level discovery, then have a look at *Chapter 9, Autodiscovery*.

Getting ready

To be able to successfully perform the steps in this recipe, you need to have a Zabbix server and a VMware server installed with some hosts already configured on the VMware server. You also need to have finished the previous recipe, *Configuring Zabbix for VMware*.

How to do it...

After we have configured Zabbix for VMware monitoring, the only thing we need to have is some patience. Next we go to **Monitoring | Latest data** and we select our VMware server from the list. After some time, Zabbix will start to fill in the data.

After waiting for the VMware discovery of our vCenter, Zabbix will start to populate the information of hypervisor and our virtual machines. Latest data grouped by hypervisor or cluster is as shown in the following screenshot:

Host	Name	Last check	Last value	Change	
	CPU (5 Items)				
	CPU cores	Nov 14th, 2013 09:03:05 AM	16	-	Graph
	CPU frequency	Nov 14th, 2013 09:03:03 AM	2 GHz	-	Graph
	CPU model	Nov 14th, 2013 09:03:04 AM	Intel(R) Xeon(R) CPU X6550 ...	-	History
	CPU threads	Nov 14th, 2013 09:03:06 AM	32	-	Graph
	CPU usage	Nov 14th, 2013 09:25:50 AM	365 MHz	+12 MHz	Graph
	Datastore (4 Items)				
	Average read latency of the datastore ...	Nov 14th, 2013 09:25:23 AM	0	-	Graph
	Average read latency of the datastore ...	Nov 14th, 2013 09:25:24 AM	0	-	Graph
	Average write latency of the datastore ...	Nov 14th, 2013 09:25:25 AM	1	-	Graph
	Average write latency of the datastore ...	Nov 14th, 2013 09:25:26 AM	0	-	Graph
	General (6 Items)				
	Cluster name	Nov 14th, 2013 09:02:57 AM	CLOUD	-	History
	Full name	Nov 14th, 2013 09:03:02 AM	VMware ESXi 5.0.0 build-9145...	-	History
	Number of guest VMs	Nov 14th, 2013 09:03:18 AM	30	-	Graph
	Overall status	Nov 14th, 2013 09:26:15 AM	1	-	Graph
	Uptime	Nov 14th, 2013 09:03:16 AM	114 days, 16:57:13	+01:00:00	Graph
	Version	Nov 14th, 2013 09:03:17 AM	5.0.0	-	History
	Hardware (4 Items)				
	Bios UUID	Nov 14th, 2013 09:03:09 AM	00000000-a602-0000-0000-0...	-	History
	Model	Nov 14th, 2013 09:03:08 AM	N20-B6730-1	-	History
	Total memory	Nov 14th, 2013 09:03:07 AM	255.95 GB	-	Graph
	Vendor	Nov 14th, 2013 09:03:10 AM	Cisco Systems Inc	-	History
	Memory (2 Items)				
	Ballooned memory	Nov 14th, 2013 09:26:11 AM	0 B	-	Graph
	Used memory	Nov 14th, 2013 09:26:12 AM	17.68 GB	-4 MB	Graph
	Network (2 Items)				
	Number of bytes received	Nov 14th, 2013 09:26:13 AM	19 KBps	-1 KBps	Graph
	Number of bytes transmitted	Nov 14th, 2013 09:26:14 AM	1 KBps	-55 KBps	Graph

Some details provided by Zabbix about a single virtual machine are seen in the following screenshot:

Name	Last check	Last value	Change
CPU (2 Items)			
CPU usage	Nov 14th, 2013 09:30:13 AM	19 MHz	-
Number of virtual CPUs	Nov 14th, 2013 09:30:12 AM	2	-
Disks (4 Items)			
Average number of kilobytes read from the disk scsi0:0	Nov 14th, 2013 09:30:53 AM	0 Bps	-
Average number of kilobytes written to the disk scsi0:0	Nov 14th, 2013 09:30:55 AM	104 KBps	-28 KBps
Average number of reads from the disk scsi0:0	Nov 14th, 2013 09:30:54 AM	0	-
Average number of writes to the disk scsi0:0	Nov 14th, 2013 09:30:56 AM	11	-4
Filesystems (8 Items)			
Free disk space on /	Nov 14th, 2013 09:30:57 AM	16.37 GB	-
Free disk space on / (percentage)	Nov 14th, 2013 09:30:59 AM	93.14 %	-
Free disk space on /boot	Nov 14th, 2013 09:30:58 AM	111.4 MB	-
Free disk space on /boot (percentage)	Nov 14th, 2013 09:31:00 AM	86.28 %	-
Total disk space on /	Nov 14th, 2013 09:19:01 AM	17.58 GB	-
Total disk space on /boot	Nov 14th, 2013 09:19:02 AM	129.11 MB	-
Used disk space on /	Nov 14th, 2013 09:31:03 AM	1.2 GB	-
Used disk space on /boot	Nov 14th, 2013 09:30:04 AM	17.71 MB	-
General (4 Items)			

How it works...

Once Zabbix is properly configured for VMware; it will access the VMware vCenter and read all information it needs from the SDK. Zabbix has some built-in templates that will be used to link automatically to the hypervisors and VMware guests.

There's more...

Note that the `Template Virt VMware` template should be used for VMware vCenter and **Elastic Sky X (ESX)** hypervisor monitoring. The `Template Virt VMware Hypervisor` and `Template Virt VMware Guest` templates are used by discovery and normally should not be manually linked to a host.

> One of the drawbacks is that Zabbix will create automatically a new guest for each VMware guest and link it to a VMware guest template. This means that if you have a Windows server or a Linux server as guest, then you still need to create a new guest and link it with the correct Linux or Windows templates. This means that each guest will be available twice in Zabbix which is not a proper solution.

There is also another option named **vPoller**; this is a community solution and is not supported by Zabbix SIA. It was developed as a solution when there was no support yet in Zabbix for VMware monitoring. Because it was developed by the community, it does certain things differently and it might be a better solution for you in certain cases.

Feature	Zabbix with vPoller	Stock Zabbix
Discovery of vSphere objects	Yes	Yes
VMware support built in Zabbix	No	Yes
VMware data center support	Yes	No
VMware clusters support	Yes	Yes
VMware Hypervisors support	Yes	Yes
VMware virtual Machine support	Yes	Yes
VMware datastore support	Yes	Basic
Is easy to extend	Yes	No
Is scalable	Yes	Yes
VMware monitoring with older Zabbix releases	Yes	No

 vPoller can be found at `http://unix-heaven.org/node/114.`

 If you would like to monitor **Kernel-based Virtual Machine** (**KVM**) with Zabbix then you could make use of the implementation that was made by another community member. This implementation will auto-discover your KVM machines and add them into Zabbix: `https://github.com/bushvin/zabbix-kvm-res.`

See also

▶ `https://www.zabbix.com/documentation/2.4/manual/vm_monitoring`

▶ `https://www.zabbix.com/documentation/2.4/manual/vm_monitoring/discovery_fields`

Installing a proxy

In this recipe, we will show you how to install a proxy in your network. The installation of a proxy is very straightforward as you will see. However, monitoring and configuring the proxy can be more complicated. For this reason, we have split up installation and the different types of configuring a proxy in this chapter.

Getting ready

What we need for this recipe is of course, our Zabbix server with super administrator rights. We need an extra machine to install our proxy.

How to do it...

As the proxy is a lightweight version of the Zabbix server, the installation procedure is almost exactly the same.

1. First we add the Zabbix repository to our server:

   ```
   rpm -ivh
   http://repo.zabbix.com/zabbix/2.4/rhel/6/x86_64/zabbix-
   release-2.4-1.el6.noarch.rpm
   ```

2. Next step is to install our `proxy`. We will make use of a SQLite database:

   ```
   yum install zabbix-proxy-sqlite3
   ```

3. Make sure the `proxy` will start at our next reboot:

   ```
   chkconfig zabbix-proxy on
   ```

4. Open the correct port in the firewall. Standardly, this is port `10051`, the same port that we use for the Zabbix trapper. Edit the `/etc/sysconfig/iptables` file and add the following line under the line with the `-dport 22` option:

   ```
   -A INPUT -m state --state NEW -m tcp -p tcp --dport 10051 -j
   ACCEPT
   ```

5. Restart the firewall:

   ```
   service iptables restart
   ```

6. Edit the `proxy` configuration by editing the `zabbix_proxy.conf` file.

   ```
   vi /etc/zabbix/zabbix_proxy.conf
   Change the following parameters
   Server=<ip of your zabbix server>
   Hostname=<name of your proxy>
   DBName=/home/zabbix/zabbix.db
   ```

7. Next step is to create the Zabbix home directory for our database:

   `mkdir /home/zabbix`

   `chmod 750 /home/zabbix`

   `chown zabbix:zabbix /home/zabbix`

8. Now we can start our Zabbix proxy:

   `service zabbix-proxy start`

9. Make sure the Zabbix proxy is running by looking at the log file:

   `tail /var/log/zabbix/zabbix_proxy.log`

10. In our Zabbix server, we now have to add our proxy. Go to **Administration | Proxies** and click on **Create** on the right of the screen. Fill in your **Proxy name** and click on **Add** button. There is no need to change anything else as yet:

11. Now go back to **Administration** | **Proxies** and after some time, you will see that the Zabbix server has some communication with the proxy.

Monitoring	Inventory	Reports	Configuration	Administration				

General | Proxies | Authentication | Users | Media types | Scripts | Audit | Queue | Notifications | Installation

History: Latest events » IT services » Configuration of IT services » IT services » Configuration of proxies

CONFIGURATION OF PROXIES

Proxies

Displaying 1 to 1 of 1 found

	Name ↑	Mode	Last seen (age)	Host count	Item count
☐	Proxy1	Active	26s	0	0

Enable selected ▼ | Go (0)

Zabbix 2.4.0 Copyright 2001-2014 by Zabbix SIA

How it works...

The Zabbix proxy is basically a Zabbix server without a graphical interface with the difference that the proxy will only collect the data and send it to the Zabbix server for processing. So when we install a proxy, we need a database just like we have on the server. In this setup, we made use of a SQLite database and as you have noticed we did not have to install anything. When you make use of a SQLite database, the proxy will create the database and do all configuration work for you.

It is possible to use any database that can be used for the Zabbix server. However, we then need to change the `zabbix_proxy.conf` file and fill in the correct username and password and tell the proxy to use a MySQLdb, PostgreSQL, or Oracle database.

Another thing that is important when using a real database is to only upload the `schema.sql` file and never the `images.sql`, and `data.sql` files!

There's more...

To monitor large or distributed networks, you can make use of Zabbix proxies. A proxy will then be responsible for a certain number of hosts. The proxy will be the only one talking to the hosts and will forward all the data to the Zabbix server.

The use of proxies is always useful when the Zabbix server cannot reach the hosts due to routing and or firewalls or for hosts in DMZ. The use of a proxy can also be used to monitor resources from outside your network.

The proxy will also reduce database load on the server when you have many hosts to monitor. Since the proxy transmits the data collected in a large block, the database needs only a few large inserts and updates processed. This produces less load than many small operations.

The combination with so-called reverse tunneling (SSH, OpenVPN) allows you to monitor with proxies on networks that can be accessed only through a connection with dynamic IP address.

A proxy can collect data on behalf of the Zabbix server. For this reason, a proxy must be compiled with the same options as the server. When you monitor, for instance, host via SNMP, then the proxy must be built with SNMP support. When you run external scripts, those scripts must be installed on the proxy instead of Zabbix server.

If you use a proxy, remember the following:

- ▶ In the configuration of the agent, you must use the proxy address as server.
- ▶ If you make use of the `zabbix_sender` option, then you must send it to the proxy.
- ▶ When you monitor a host by proxy, all checks are performed by the proxy. It is not possible to run individual checks from the server.
- ▶ If you are using external scripts on the server, all scripts must also be stored on the proxy.
- ▶ Configurations that you make on the server through the web GUI reach the proxies with delay.
- ▶ Zabbix server and proxy should be the same version. Expect problems if the proxy has a different version than the server.
- ▶ Zabbix server and proxy can use different databases. The data exchange is not at the database level. You can use, for example, PostgreSQL for the Zabbix server and SQLite for proxies.
- ▶ A SQLite database should be able to handle about + / - 50 hosts; it depends on how many items you monitor and the interval at which you check them and on the hardware. It should even be possible to archive about 500 VPS.
- ▶ The requirements for a proxy are very low and could even run on embedded hardware. (Have a look on the Zabbix forum for some projects):
    - ❑ https://www.zabbix.com/forum/showthread.php?t=21430.
    - ❑ https://www.zabbix.com/forum/showthread.php?t=36867&high light=raspberry.

See also

- ▶ https://www.zabbix.com/documentation/2.4/manual/appendix/ install/db_scripts

Setting up an active proxy

Just as with agents in Zabbix, we have proxies that can be active or passive. In this recipe, we will explain you how to configure the proxy as an active proxy and we will show you what parameters are important.

Getting ready

What we need for this recipe is of course, our Zabbix server with super administrator rights. We need an extra machine to install our proxy. You also have to set up your proxy as we showed you in the previous recipe, *Installing a proxy*.

How to do it...

1. Set up your proxy as in the previous recipe, *Installing a proxy*.

2. Make sure that in the `zabbix_proxy.conf` file, the option `ProxyMode=0` is set.

3. Be sure to fill in the IP address of your Zabbix server under the option `Server` in the `zabbix_proxy.conf` file.

4. Also fill in the `Hostname` in the same `conf` file.

5. Have a look at the options `ConfigFrequency` and `DataSenderFrequency` as these two options will determine how many times the proxy will go look for a new configuration on the Zabbix server and how many times the proxy sends the collected data from the hosts to the Zabbix server:

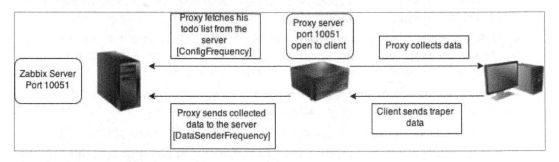

How it works...

When making use of an active proxy, it is the proxy that logs in to the server. The proxy must connect to the server on port 10051. The server does not have access to the proxy. An active proxy can be used when the proxy uses a dynamic IP address.

There's more...

The settings relating to the accessibility are not handled from the server but from the proxy. Don't forget to check the following settings in the `zabbix_proxy.conf` file, and possibly align it with your settings from Zabbix server:

`UnreachablePeriod`, `UnavailableDelay`, and `UnreachableDelay`.

See also

▶ https://www.zabbix.com/documentation/2.4/manual/appendix/config/zabbix_proxy

Setting up a passive proxy

In this recipe, we will show you how to set up your passive proxy. We will also show you the most important parameters that you need to configure when setting up a passive proxy.

Getting ready

What we need for this recipe is of course, our Zabbix server with super administrator rights. We need an extra machine to install our proxy. You also have to set up your proxy as we showed you in the previous recipe, *Installing a proxy*.

How to do it...

1. Install the Zabbix proxy just as we have seen in the recipe, *Installing a proxy*.

2. In the `zabbix_proxy.conf` file, we need to change the option `Proxy Mode`:

    `Proxy Mode = 1`

3. Change the `ProxyConfigFrequency = 3600` option in the `zabbix_server.conf` file to a value that suits this option. This will influence how many times the Zabbix server will send the configuration to the proxy.

4. Change the `ProxyDataFrequency = 1` option in the `zabbix_server.conf` file to a value that suits you. This will tell the Zabbix server how many times it needs to fetch history data from the proxy.

5. In the `zabbix_server.conf` file, alter the option `StartProxyPollers=1` to at least the number of proxies in your network.

6. Restart both Zabbix server and proxy to update the configuration.

7. `service zabbix-server restart` and for the proxy `service zabbix-proxy restart`.

8. Go to the Zabbix web frontend to **Administration | Proxies** and create a proxy.

9. Add the **Proxy name**.

10. Select `Passive` for **Proxy mode**.

11. Add the correct **Interface** (IP or DNS preferable IP).

12. Save the configuration.

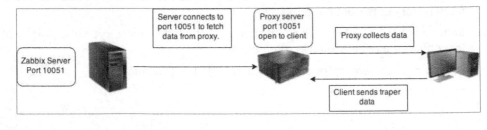

How it works...

When we work with a passive proxy, the proxy will just work like a passive client. The proxy will wait for the server to initiate a connection to fetch all the data from the proxy.

A passive proxy is perfect to use in a DMZ zone where you don't just want your severs to communicate with your LAN. This way the Zabbix server will initiate the connection and fetch all data from the proxy over port 10051.

See also

▶ https://www.zabbix.com/documentation/2.4/manual/appendix/
config/zabbix_proxy

Monitoring hosts through a proxy

After setting up a proxy, we want to add some hosts to our proxy. In this recipe, we will show you how to link your hosts to the installed proxies.

Getting ready

For this recipe, we need our Zabbix server with an active or passive proxy configured like we have done in one of the previous recipes. We also need a host that we can use to connect to our proxy.

How to do it...

Adding a host to a proxy is a very straightforward method and doesn't take much time:

1. First we have to change the `Server` and/or `ActiveServer` values in the configuration of our Zabbix client. This can be done in the `zabbix_agentd.conf` configuration file. Instead of the Zabbix server's IP we add the IP of our proxy.

2. Restart the agent:

   ```
   service zabbix-proxy restart
   ```

3. In the Zabbix server, go to the agent in the menu **Configuration | Hosts**. Select the correct host and at the bottom of the host page, select from Monitored by proxy the correct proxy from the list.

4. Now, go to **Administration | Proxies**. You will see that the **Host count** and **Item count** has increased.

Name	Mode	Last seen (age)	Host count	Item count	Required performance (vps)
Proxy1	Passive	3s	1	44	0.52

The proxy will also show the number of items and the required **Virtual Private Server** (VPS).

How it works...

As we have seen in our schemas, once a proxy is in place, the host(s) will only communicate with the proxy once the host is configured correctly. From that moment, the proxy will act as Zabbix server so everything that was done from the Zabbix server will be done from the proxy from now on. So if we want to monitor for example, IPMI, we will have to install the correct libraries on our proxy. If we want to run external scripts, then we need to install them on the proxy instead of the Zabbix server.

There's more...

Triggers are always evaluated by Zabbix server. The proxy will only collect the data and give it to the Zabbix server. It is very important once you set up proxies that you make use of the NTP server so that the time between Zabbix server, proxies, and hosts is always OK!

Don't forget that the `ProxyConfigFrequency=3600` option is standard. That means, that if you change something on the proxy, the proxy will only be notified of those changes after 3600 seconds. The next command example will reload the configuration cache so that the active proxy will ask the server for the latest configuration:

```
zabbix_proxy -c /etc/zabbix/zabbix_proxy.conf -R
config_cache_reload
```

See also

 ▸   https://www.zabbix.com/documentation/2.0/manual/concepts/proxy

Monitoring the proxy

Having a proxy is nice, but how do you know that your proxy is still running fine? Are the buffers big enough? Do we need to optimize certain settings? And probably most importantly, how do you know when your proxy is not reporting any data? In this recipe, I will show you the answers to those questions.

Getting ready

What do we need ? As usual, we need our Zabbix server with super administration rights and of course, a Zabbix proxy properly configured as we have seen in the recipes setting up an active or a passive proxy.

How to do it...

1. The first thing we have to do is set up an item on our Zabbix server. Go to **Configuration | Hosts** and create an item on your proxy.

2. Use the following parameters to create your item:

   ❑ **Type**: Zabbix internal

   ❑ **Key**: zabbix [proxy, <proxy name>, lastaccess]

   ❑ **Type of information**: Numeric (unsigned)

   ❑ **Data type**: Decimal

   ❑ **Units**: unixtime

CONFIGURATION OF ITEMS

« Host list   **Host:** Zabbix server   Enabled   🔲🔲🔲🔲   Applications (12)   Items (75)   Triggers (45)   Graphs (13)   Discovery rules (2)

Item

Name	Proxy $2 Last access time
Type	Zabbix internal ▼
Key	zabbix[proxy,Proxy1,lastacces] Select
Type of information	Numeric (unsigned) ▼
Data type	Decimal ▼
Units	unixtime
Use custom multiplier	☐ 1
Update interval (in sec)	30
Flexible intervals	**Interval** **Period** **Action** No flexible intervals defined.
New flexible interval	Interval (in sec) 50 Period 1-7,00:00-24:00 Add

⊟ Proxy (1 Item)		
☐ Proxy Proxy1 Last access time	2014-12-14 10:12:51	2014-12-14 10:12:49

3. When you now look at the latest data, you will see the last access time from your proxy on the Zabbix server.

4. The next thing we have to do is set up up a trigger for our item. Go to **Configuration | Hosts** and click on **Triggers** on the Zabbix server.

5. Create a new trigger with an expression like this:

```
{Zabbix
server:zabbix[proxy,Proxy1,lastaccess].fuzzytime(180)}=0
```

6. Now after 180 seconds of no response, we will get a warning that there is an issue with our proxy.

Trigger	Dependencies

Name | Proxy1 has not synced with {HOST.HOST} for some time !

Expression | {Zabbix server:zabbix[proxy,Proxy1,lastaccess].fuzzytime(180)}=0 | Add

Expression constructor

Multiple PROBLEM events generation ☐

Description

URL

Severity | Not classified | Information | Warning | Average | **High** | Disaster

Enabled ☑

How it works...

In case of active proxy, it will be the proxy sending an heartbeat to the Zabbix server to report that he is still online. In case of passive proxy, it will be the Zabbix server checking for the proxy. Our trigger will look into both cases for the latest time the proxy was reached or had reported that it was still available and check how long it has been. In our case, the alarm will be sent after 180 seconds.

There's more...

The proxy reports to the Zabbix server with some kind of heartbeat. Make sure you check the configuration from the proxy, so that it reports in regular times to the Zabbix server. For the active proxy, this is the option `HeartbeatFrequency` and for the passive proxy, you can look in the Zabbix server configuration for the option `ProxyDataFrequency`.

Zabbix has provided us with a special template for the proxy, `Template App Zabbix Proxy`. Linking this template will show you the inner health of the proxy. Here you will be able to see if buffers are too small or if we need more pollers and so on. Another option to monitor your proxy can be the installation of a full Zabbix client.

9
Autodiscovery

In this chapter, we will cover the following topics:

- ▸ Configuring network discovery
- ▸ Automation after discovery
- ▸ Active agent auto-registration
- ▸ Low-level discovery

Introduction

Zabbix, as we have seen so far, is a nice tool for monitoring and is very flexible. However, configuring Zabbix can be a real daunting task. Zabbix has created some tools that we can use to make our life much easier by automating things. In this chapter, we will see how to automate certain aspects in Zabbix.

Configuring network discovery

When we want to do some automation in our network, the first thing that we have to do is the configuration of the network discovery tool in Zabbix. This way we can detect devices in our network based on some pre-defined settings such as devices with certain services active, pingable, and so on. In this recipe, we will show you how to configure the network discovery tool. Later we will show you how to automate things based on the discovery tool.

Getting ready

For this recipe to work, we need a Zabbix server with an administrator account or a super admin account.

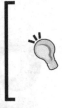

Before Zabbix 2.4.4 IP range matching was possible by specifying a range like 192.168.1.1-255. That however, was not sufficient for easily specifying multiple subnets.

Since Zabbix 2.4.4 the range option has now been extended to also allow specifying a range like 192.168.1-10.1-255.

How to do it...

1. Go in the Zabbix menu to **Configuration | Discovery**.

2. Click **Create discovery rule** or edit the existing one.

3. Give a Name, for example, the name of your network (LAN, DMZ, MGMT).

4. In the **Discovered by proxy** box, you can select if you would like the discovery to be done by a proxy.

5. In the box **IP range**, we have to put the range of the network that we would like to scan. We can make use of a CIDR notation here such as 192.168.0.1/24, or just as in the example define the range such as 192.168.0.1-254 or we can just add a single IP.

6. The delay is defined in seconds in the box **Delay (in sec)** and is the number of seconds Zabbix will initiate a new scan after the first scan is finished.

7. In the box **Checks**, we can define certain checks that Zabbix will use for the discovery of the devices on the network.

8. The **Device uniqueness criteria** box is where we can select how to make sure we will not have one device multiple times in our discovery list.

9. **Enabled** will activate our discovery rule or keep it disabled.

10. Once you update the details, click on **Update** to update the rule. Also, in case you have similar rule, then you can use the **Clone** option to clone and change IP range or other details accordingly.

How it works

When creating a discovery rule, Zabbix will scan the network range given in our configuration for hosts that can be reached based on our checks that we have defined. For this to work, you need to make sure that the subnet is reachable by Zabbix as the Zabbix server obviously cannot route to networks by itself.

Once a device is discovered, Zabbix will create an event. You can go to **Monitoring | Events** and select **Discovery** from the dropdown box under **Source** on the top right.

There is more...

Since Zabbix 2.2.0, the hosts discovered by different proxies are always treated as different hosts. Discovery will not do much by itself and you would probably want to create some actions later based on the discovery rules you made. It's probably best to keep your discovery rules disabled until your action is created, as actions will be launched once events are generated.

Zabbix will periodically scan the IP ranges that were defined in network discovery rules. The frequency at which Zabbix does this is configurable for each rule individually. However every rule will only use one process.

Remember that the delay in seconds is the amount of time Zabbix will wait to start the next scan once the first scan is finished. This way, you will not initiate too much unneeded traffic on your network.

See also

▶ https://www.zabbix.com/documentation/2.4/manual/discovery/network_discovery/rule

Automation after discovery

After we have done some discovery of our devices on the network, it's time to do something with our discovered items. In this recipe, we will show you how to create some devices in Zabbix after we have discovered them.

Getting ready

For this recipe to work, we need our Zabbix server with already configured network discovery such as in the previous recipe, *Configuring network discovery*. And of course, we also need a device that can be discovered on our network. For this recipe, it's ok if we can ping our device.

How to do it...

1. Go to **Configuration | Actions** and select **Discovery** from the **Event source** dropdown on the top right.

2. Create a new action by pressing the **Create action** button on the top right corner.

3. Now we have to configure our **Action**. First, we just give our action a **Name** in the **Action** tab.

4. Then we have to add a condition for our action in the **Conditions** tab. Here we will add a simple condition that says Discovery status = Discovered.

5. In our **Operations** tab, we have to add the operation we expect Zabbix to perform once the discovery has finished and our conditions were met. Here we keep it simple and tell Zabbix to **Add** host and click on **Update** button.

6. After some time when you see in the event page that devices are discovered, go to the **Hosts** tab and you will see some new devices in your host list.

How it works

In our **Actions** tab, we have defined a new action for the event source **Discovery**. Zabbix presented us 3 different tabs. In the first tab, we only filled the name of our action but we can do more. We can tell Zabbix to inform us by mail when an action was launched and for this, we can make use of the **Default message** box and **Default subject** box to inform us with the details we want to know. Look in the *See also* section for a URL that points to the list of macros that can be used.

The next tab that we had to fill in was the **Conditions** tab, where we have defined the condition Zabbix had to check before doing our operation. Our condition here was to look if the device was discovered. More complex things can be done here. We can look, for example, for devices in certain IP ranges or for certain kernel versions or only for devices that have FTP or SNMP ports enabled. It's a good practice in general to look for a certain uptime or downtime before adding to or removing a device from Zabbix.

In the **Operations tab**, we have told Zabbix what to do once the device was discovered and in the example we have told Zabbix to add the host. Once again more complex things can be done here, such as sending a message, linking it to a template, removing a host or even launching a custom script, and so on.

There is more...

Make sure that the network discovery is properly configured and still on DISABLED. This is very important because our registration will only work once an event is created. It's better to configure all the actions and then enable network discovery, else you will have to wait till new events are created.

See also

- ▸ https://www.zabbix.com/documentation/2.4/manual/appendix/macros/supported_by_location
- ▸ https://www.zabbix.com/documentation/2.4/manual/discovery/network_discovery/rule

Active agent autoregistration

Another way to do some automation in Zabbix is to automate the registration of active clients. It is possible to register an active Zabbix client automatically in the Zabbix server once it is detected.

Getting ready

For this recipe to work, we need our Zabbix server with administrator rights and of course a Zabbix agent that is configured to be an active agent. Make sure that the agent is set up and not added to the Zabbix server yet, as this is what we will automate in this recipe. In production, this will be an added value as we can automate in Zabbix the discovery and configuration of new hosts in our environment. For instance, when an administrator installs new servers with a golden image or with some configuration management tools, the server will automatically be detected by the Zabbix server and / or added to a group and linked with a template.

How to do it ...

1. In the Zabbix menu, go to **Configuration | Actions** and select **Auto registration** as the **Event source** from the dropdown on the upper right.

2. Press the **Create action** button just preceding the **Event source** box.

3. In the **Action** box just fill in the **Name**.

4. In the **Condition** tab, we can specify the condition. This is optional and we will skip it in this recipe. You can make use of this if you want to specify the HostMetadata or HostMetadataItem from the agents configuration file but this is optional.

5. In the **Operations** tab, we will add the relevant operation in our case it will be Add host.

6. Press the **Add** button to add the new rule to the **Actions** page.

![Zabbix Configuration of Actions screen showing the Action tab with Name "Add new clients", Default subject "Auto registration: {HOST.HOST}", Default message listing Host name, Host IP, Agent port, and an Enabled checkbox, with Update, Clone, Delete, and Cancel buttons]

7. Once you update all the details, click the **Update** button.

How it works

The automatic agent registration works only with active agents, so we need to make sure that in the zabbix_agentd.conf file the option ServerActive= is filled in with the address of our Zabbix server (or proxy).

We have to create an action just as we do with the network discovery; however it is not needed to do any network discovery in this case.

In the **Action** we have defined a new name for our action and we could add a subject and a message to inform us, for example by email, once an agent has been registered.

In the **Conditions** tab, we have not added anything but it would be possible to filter for only certain hostnames, host metadata, or proxies.

In the **Operations** tab we told Zabbix to add the host to Zabbix once conditions were met. Here we have many more options. We could also send a message, add the host to a group, link it with a template, launch a remote command, and so on.

There is more...

To get information for the host metadata we have to configure this data in the `zabbix_agentd.conf` file. There are two lines in the `agent` configuration file `HostMetadata` and `HostMetadataItem` that can be used for this. This can be useful if you would like to define certain servers as, for example, web servers, database servers, and so on.

> It's in general a good practice not to add and remove clients when discovered or when not discovered anymore, as a host may be unreachable or an agent can be installed on a temporary machine. It's probably wise to use a certain delay before an action is taken.
>
> Zabbix states that an auto-registration attempt happens every time an active agent sends a request to refresh the active checks to the server. The delay between requests is specified in the `RefreshActiveChecks` parameter of the Zabbix agent. The first request will be sent immediately after the agent is restarted.

See also

- https://www.zabbix.com/documentation/2.4/manual/appendix/macros/supported_by_location
- https://www.zabbix.com/documentation/2.4/manual/discovery/auto_registration

Low-level discovery

In Zabbix, another way to automate is to make use of low-level discovery. This way Zabbix can automatically create items, triggers, and graphs. At the moment, there are four types in Zabbix that can be discovered out of the box. Zabbix is able to discover filesystems, network interfaces, CPUs, cores, and SNMP OIDs.

Getting ready

For this recipe, we will need our Zabbix server and a Zabbix linux host. The Zabbix host just needs to be properly installed and added to the Zabbix server, but without any templates linked to the hst. On the Zabbix server we need administrator rights.

How to do it ...

1. The first thing to do is to go to **Configuration | Hosts or Templates | Discovery rules**.
2. Click on the **Create discovery** rule button on the upper right.
3. Add a **Name** for our rule: Mounted File System Discovery.
4. Select the **Type** Zabbix agent (active).
5. Add the **Key**; in this case, the key is vfs.fs.discovery.
6. Select an **Update interval** 60 (in production, this could be once a day or an hour).
7. In the **Filters** tab, add the **Macro** {#FSTYPE} with **Regular expression** @File systems for discovery. (We explain this later in *How it works*):

8. Add a nice **Description** and press the **Add** button in the **Discovery rule** tab.
9. Once you update all the details, click on the **Update** button which saves your changes. Now we can create an item by clicking on **Item prototypes**:

10. Click on the **Create item prototype** button.
11. Add a **Name** for the **Item prototype**.
12. Select a **Type**: Zabbix agent (active).
13. Add a **Key**, in our case, this is vfs.fs.size[{#FSNAME},pfree].
14. Add the **Type of information**: Numeric (float).
15. Add the **Unit**: in %.
16. Add a **Description** and press the **Add** button.

17. Now, if we wait a bit and go to **Monitoring | Latest data**, we will see that Zabbix has detected the filesystems on our host and the percentage free space on those filesystems.

	Last check	Last value
Filesystem (2 items)		
Free diskspace on / (Percentage)	2014-12-20 12:42:43	82.33 %
Free diskspace on /boot (Percentage)	2014-12-20 12:42:43	93.05 %

How it works

The first thing we did was create a discovery rule to tell Zabbix what to discover. This could be a filesystem, network interface, CPU, CPU cores, or an SNMP device. In our case, it was a filesystem.

We added a filter. This filter was already defined in Zabbix so we just had to point to this filter. Filters can be made by making use of regular expressions. You can check out the filter we have used under **Administration | General | Regular expressions**.

There are already some filters defined for filesystems, network interfaces, and SNMP storage devices. Once our discovery rule was defined and our filter was added we made an item prototype. An item prototype will tell Zabbix what items it has to discover. In our item prototype, we made use of the **macro** `{#FSNAME}` in our key instead of the name of our filesystem. For example: `/`, `/usr`, `/var`, and so on.

There's more...

Once an item is not discovered anymore, it will receive an orange indication with an exclamation mark in the items list. When you hover your mouse over, it will show you how much time is left before the item will be removed from the items list. This time can be set in the option **Keep lost resources period (in days)** in the general **Discovery rule**.

7	365	Zabbix agent	Filesystems	Not supported	
The item is not discovered anymore and will be deleted in 29d 23h 35m (on 2015-03-02 at 14:27).					
7	365	Zabbix agent	Filesystems	Enabled	
7	365	Zabbix agent	Filesystems	Enabled	

Since Zabbix 2.4, it is possible to add more than one filter. Earlier, one could add just one filter in a low-level discovery rule.

A user can also define his or her own types of discovery. For this to work, you have to follow a particular JSON protocol. More information with examples on how to do this can be found in the Zabbix documentation.

See also

▸ https://www.zabbix.com/documentation/2.4/manual/discovery/low_
level_discovery

10
Zabbix Maintenance and API

In this chapter, we will cover the following recipes:

- Maintenance periods
- Monitoring Zabbix
- Backups
- Avoiding performance issues
- Zabbix API
- API by example

Introduction

So far we have seen how to set up Zabbix to get information from our hosts and to get notified when things go wrong. In this chapter, I will try to show you how to do some maintenance tasks in Zabbix and explain you how to improve the performance. We will also have a quick look at the API.

Maintenance periods

In Zabbix, it is possible to create a maintenance period for the times we need to do some maintenance on our servers. It would be awkward to get a bunch of notifications when we know that our servers are down for a certain period of time. In Zabbix we can split maintenance periods in two major types, maintenance with and without data collection.

Getting ready

For this recipe, we need our Zabbix server with administrator rights. We also need at least one host set up and added in our Zabbix configuration. We will make use of this host to show you how to add a host or a group in maintenance period.

How to do it...

1. Go to the Zabbix menu to **Configuration | Maintenance**.

2. Click on **Create maintenance period** to see the window as shown in the following screenshot:

3. Fill in a **Name** for our maintenance period.

4. Select the **Maintenance type:** No data collection.

5. Select the **Active since** date.

6. Select the **Active till** date.

7. Add a **Description** so that people know why there is a maintenance foreseen.

8. Click on the **Periods** tab to view the window seen in the following screenshot:

9. Select from the **Period type** box if the maintenance has to happen one time, Daily, Weekly, or Monthly. In this example, I have chosen Weekly.

10. In **Every week(s)**, we fill in if it has to happen every week or every 2 weeks. Similarly, if you have chosen days, it will be every day or every 2 days and so on.

11. Select the **Day of the week** or the months if you have selected months.

12. In the **At (hour:minute)** box, you can give the time at which the maintenance period has to start.

13. In **Maintenance period length**, you add how long the maintenance window has to last.

14. Next go to the tab **Hosts & Groups**.

15. Select what host or what group you want to maintain and click on **Add**.

16. When we go to **Configuration | Hosts**, we will see that our host is In maintenance mode:

How it works...

From the **Maintenance** tab, we have selected the start and the end day of our maintenance period. We also told Zabbix to collect or not collect data.

We then went to the **Periods** tab. In this tab, we were able to do some more fine-tuning in our maintenance schedule, for example, recurring periods on a weekly basis.

From our **Periods** tab, we went to the **Hosts & Groups** tab where we selected all hosts and / or host groups that we wanted to place in maintenance.

There's more...

During a maintenance period `With data collection`, Zabbix will process triggers and create events as usual. So when we reboot servers or shutdown services, we will get notified about those events. If you would like to skip notifications during the maintenance period, then we have to put the `Maintenance status = not in maintenance` in the trigger action by navigating to **Configuration | Actions | Triggers**.

If a trigger generates an event during the maintenance period, then once the maintenance period has ended, an additional event will be created. This is to make sure that if a problem happened during the maintenance period, you will get notified about the problem if it is not resolved even after the maintenance period is over.

Remember that there are two types of maintenance periods:

`With data collection`: Data will be collected by the server during maintenance, triggers will be processed, and event will be created.

`No data collection`: Data will not be collected by the server during maintenance period. Last check in latest data will stay at the same time.

See also

► `https://www.zabbix.com/documentation/2.4/manual/maintenance`

Monitoring Zabbix

When you run Zabbix, it's not always easy to know how many pollers you need, for example for SNMP, IPMI, and so on. To find out more about this, Zabbix has some built-in health checks. In this topic, we will show you how to read them.

Getting ready

For this recipe, make sure that you are a Zabbix administrator and that you have your agent configured on the Zabbix server. Also make sure that the template `Template App Zabbix Server` is linked with your Zabbix host.

How to do it

From the menu, go to **Monitoring** | **Latest data** and select the **Zabbix server** as host to see. Select Zabbix server from the item list to get an overiew of the data of all items:

	Zabbix server (30 Items)		
	Values processed by Zabbix server per second	2015-01-31 16:50:57	0.9
	Zabbix busy alerter processes, in %	2015-01-31 16:50:32	0 %
	Zabbix busy configuration syncer processes, in %	2015-01-31 16:50:33	0.05 %
	Zabbix busy db watchdog processes, in %	2015-01-31 16:50:34	0.02 %
	Zabbix busy discoverer processes, in %	2015-01-31 16:50:35	0.07 %
	Zabbix busy escalator processes, in %	2015-01-31 16:50:36	0.02 %
	Zabbix busy history syncer processes, in %	2015-01-31 16:50:37	0.09 %

Here we have an easy overview of how much our pollers are busy or idle. Remember that in our Zabbix 2.4, we have graphs automatically generated in **Latest data**, so we can click on those graphs and see easy if, for example, at a certain time pollers were not enough available.

The data that we see here is based on the internal items, more specifically this one: `zabbix[process,<type>,<mode>,<state>]`.

With this item, we first have to choose a process type that we want to monitor. We select a type from a long list.. Here we specify what we want to monitor, be it a trapper, ICMP pinger, housekeeper, or anything else.

Next we specify the mode. The mode will tell us what data we want to see from our process, for example .avg, max, min, and so on.

And as last option, we specify the state from our process. Here we will specify if we want to monitor the busy or idle state from our process.

For a full list of types that can be used, check the Zabbix documentation and look for `zabbix[process,<type>,<mode>,<state>]`.

`https://www.zabbix.com/documentation/2.4/manual/config/items/itemtypes/internal`.

See also

- `http://blog.zabbix.com/monitoring-how-busy-zabbix-processes-are/457/`

Backups

Once you have your Zabbix server up and running, it's important to back up your Zabbix configuration in case you should run into problems. In this topic, we will cover what we need to backup and how to do it. While it's not really a recipe on how to backup as each Zabbix set up is different and not everybody uses MySQL or PostgreSQL, we will show you how to run your backups.

Getting ready

For this recipe to work, all we need is a working Zabbix server with a MySQL database.

How to do it...

In the **crontab** of your server, add the following line:

```
1 0 * * *  mysqldump -u <user> -p<password> <zabbixdb> >
/backup/zabbix_db_backup
```

How it works...

This recipe showed a basic backup of the MySQL database of our Zabbix server. When we backup Zabbix, it depends on what database we have used to do our backup. To avoid locking, it is possible to make use of tools such as **Percona XtraBackup**. When you work with PostgreSQL, you could make use of the **pg_dump** utility.

The database is the most important backup in Zabbix, as all information is stored in the database. In this example, we have a backup running every night 1 minute after midnight to the volume / backup. This volume can be a volume mounted on a different server or NAS.

There's more...

This backup solution is not perfect but works in small Zabbix setups. It's actually far from perfect as it will create some heavy loads in bigger setups. For those setups, there are other solutions, such as database replication or a dump excluding the history and the trends table as it's the tables that take up a lot of space and time to dump.

Another solution could be to write a small script that does the database dump and checks if the dump was OK and monitor this output with Zabbix to get notified in case of issues.

Also important to remember is to backup your frontend files in case you have tweaked your frontend. Another important thing to backup is your `zabbix_server.conf` file as it will probably change during time. Same goes for the agents and the proxy servers in your network.

The backup of those files is not a Zabbix job. For this, you have your trustworthy backup softwares such as Zmanda, Bacula, and so on. However, it could be useful to create your script so that it collects all files in one `.tar.gz` file.

If you make use of **mysqldump** program, make sure you add some options such as `--single-transaction` to avoid database locking. Having a backup of your `externalscripts` directory can come in handy.

Making a backup of your templates by exporting them in Zabbix can also be easy later when you want to install a new Zabbix server or a Zabbix server for testing.

See also

 ▸ A few scripts that will make your life easier when you want to automate your database backup:

 ❑ `http://www.zmanda.com/quick-mysql-backup.html`

 ❑ `http://sourceforge.net/projects/automysqlbackup/`

 ❑ `https://wiki.postgresql.org/wiki/Automated_Backup_on_Linux`

Avoiding performance issues

Once you have mastered Zabbix and your installation is up and running, there are probably some performance issues that will pop up over time. In this recipe, we will try to show you how to tweak your Zabbix for the best possible performance. Once again this is not really a recipe as not every Zabbix server is the same, but useful to check and remember when you install Zabbix.

Getting ready

For this all we need is a running Zabbix installation. We don't need to have performance issues but if you have them, I hope we can solve them with our guidelines and tips.

How to do it...

When you install Zabbix, make sure you always have the latest version of Zabbix. Each version released over the years has had major improvements; so it's very useful to update for performance considerations if not for the new features.

Upgrade your database! It doesn't matter if you run on PostgreSQL or MySQL or anything else. Databases improve and especially for MySQL, major improvements were made in the latest versions and for PostgreSQL since 8.x version. Don't stay with the version that comes with your distribution. Also **MariaDB** an or **PerconaDB** could be good alternatives. Of course always check if the version is supported by Zabbix.

If possible, buy **Solid-state Drive** (**SSD**) drives for the database. This will increase the NVPS dramatically that Zabbix can write into the database. If SSD is still too slow for your set up, try **PCIe SSD** disk if you can afford the price tag that comes with it.

Check your items interval and make sure you don't check every 30 seconds where you don't need to check. Remember Zabbix will put everything in a database. Checking too aggressively can not only bring down your Zabbix server but also your hosts. For example, checking all ports on a switch every 30 seconds for all parameters won't do much good to your Zabbix server and especially to your switch.

The number of items you monitor can also be an issue if you monitor too many things. It will take up resources that you can use for other items.

Remember points 4 and 5 and then look at the templates and delete or disable all items you don't need and change the intervals. Standard templates in Zabbix are mostly ok for small setups but too aggressive to be useful in larger environments.

Make use of proxies where it's possible to take away some load of the database. Remember the proxy will collect all data and then send it in one batch to the Zabbix server or the Zabbix server will collect it every x number of seconds. Proxies will also do other tasks such as SNMP and IPMI monitoring. (`https://www.zabbix.com/documentation/2.4/manual/distributed_monitoring/proxies`).

Make use of active items as much as possible. Remember the Zabbix server will contact agents to ask for the data in case of passive agents. Making use of an active agent will take this load away as the active agent collects all data and sends it to the Zabbix server. The active agent also has a buffer, so data will be sent in big blocks reducing the write jobs to the database.

Making use of a dedicated database server can also be a huge advantage as the disks will be dedicated to the database only.

Avoid **Redundant Array of Independent Disks** (**RAID**) 3,4,5, and 6 for your databases! RAID 1+ 0 is probably a good choice but expensive. Also stay away from software raid and make use of battery-backed RAID controllers.

Do some database tweaking. The standard configuration of your database is not made for optimal performance and is different for each setup. There are some handy tools that can tweak your database such as **MySQLTuner-perl** or **PgTune**. Check the *See also* section of this recipe for links to those tools.

Tune Apache just as you tuned your database. Don't know where to start? Take a look in the *See also* section where I have added a few URLs to get you started.

Add lots of RAM; the more RAM you have the better. It would be perfect if the database fits in your RAM).

Another solution used in bigger setups is making use of database partitioning. This way historical data can be split up, for example, per month instead of keeping everything in one big table. This makes looking up data more quick, also backing up will be faster as we only have to back up the latest data. For information on how to do this, look at `www.zabbix.org`. Here you will find some guides on how to partition your PostgreSQL or MySQL database.

Check housekeeper; make sure it's not busy all the time or removing too much data for a long period.

Tune your templates, don't gather data every 10 seconds on every item and don't keep data longer then needed in the history and trends database.

Triggers with `min`, `max`, and `avg` are slower than `last()` and `nodata()` functions as Zabbix needs to calculate this data. Avoid them if not needed.

Polling data by SNMP, agent less or passive agents is slower compared to traps and active agents.

Text and string data types are slower to process than numeric data types.

See also

- `http://www.baarf.com/`
- `http://mysqltuner.com/`
- `https://wiki.postgresql.org/wiki/Performance_Optimization`
- `http://pgtune.leopard.in.ua/`
- `http://pgtune.projects.pgfoundry.org/`
- `http://dev.mysql.com/doc/refman/5.1/en/mysqldump.html`
- `https://github.com/Trikke76/Bash-Scripts/blob/master/Apachebuddy.pl`
- `https://github.com/Trikke76/Bash-Scripts/blob/master/apache-tuner.sh`

Zabbix API

Once you have your Zabbix server up and running, you would probably like to integrate it in the rest of your infrastructure. This is where the Zabbix API comes into picture. By using the API, we can extend Zabbix and integrate it with our other solutions. In this chapter, we will show you how to connect to the API and explain you the basics to interact with it.

Getting ready

In this recipe, we only need our Zabbix server with the super administration account.

How to do it...

1. Make sure you have curl on your system. It should be there when you installed your system. If not run:

   ```
   yum install curl
   ```

2. Run the following command on your Zabbix server's prompt or from another machine but then replace the IP:

   ```
   curl -s -i -X POST -H 'Content-Type: application/json-rpc' -d
   '{ "params": { "user": "<user>", "password": "<password>" },
   "jsonrpc": "2.0", "method": "user.login", "id": 0 }'
   'http://127.0.0.1/zabbix/api_jsonrpc.php'
   ```

   The output should look more or less like the following lines:

   ```
   HTTP/1.1 200 OK

   Date: Sat, 27 Dec 2014 12:43:31 GMT

   Server: Apache/2.2.15 (CentOS)

   X-Powered-By: PHP/5.3.3

   Access-Control-Allow-Origin: *

   Access-Control-Allow-Headers: Content-Type

   Access-Control-Allow-Methods: POST

   Access-Control-Max-Age: 1000

   Content-Length: 68

   Connection: close

   Content-Type: application/json
   ```

   ```
   {"jsonrpc":"2.0","result":"b58610b7bc18ea8579e8d03e38dee665","
   id":0}
   ```

How it works...

We made use of curl to send a simplified JSON request to the Zabbix API. To be successful in our request, we had to specify some parameters. First, we specified the protocol: `"jsonrpc": "2.0"`. We also had to specify the `"method"` parameter. This parameter will tell Zabbix what we want to do, for example, create a host or an item or add a template; we made use of the `user.login` option. With the `params` option we were able to specify our login and password to log into the API. The `id` parameter is a field that is being used to tie a JSON request to its response so that each response will have the same ID.

From Zabbix, we then received the authentication information back in a JSON format. `"result"`: the authentication token that we can use to identify us in our next tasks. And the `"id"` parameter that belongs to this response. The `id` is an arbitrary identifier of the request that was made by us.

There's more...

The Zabbix API was added to Zabbix since version 1.8 and has evolved since then in every version. Since Zabbix 2.0, we can say that the API has been stable. So it's very important that if you write some code, you know what version of Zabbix you are using. Make sure you check what has been changed in the API before you upgrade Zabbix as things may be broken after the upgrade.

If you make use of a Zabbix server where frontend, database, and backend are split, then remember that the Zabbix API runs on the frontend.

A reference of all methods that can be used when programming can be found here: `https://www.zabbix.com/documentation/2.4/manual/api/reference`.

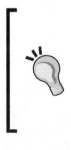

It's probably wise to create a special user for the Zabbix API and to remember that it's better to use HTTPS than HTTP, else passwords and logins will be send unencrypted.

To make life more easy when programming the API, Zabbix provides us a list of third-party libraries that can work with the API. Those libraries can be used in Python, PHP, Ruby, and so on. Check See also for a URL with a full list of libraries.

Zabbix adds for every method, examples to show you how to use the API. Those are based on the PHP language.

For example, here we see how to add a host to Zabbix by making use of the host.create method.

`https://www.zabbix.com/documentation/2.4/manual/api/reference/host/create`.

See also

- http://zabbix.org/wiki/Docs/api/libraries
- https://www.zabbix.com/documentation/2.4/manual/api/changes_2.2_-_2.4
- https://www.zabbix.com/documentation/2.4/manual/api

API by example

As it's always easier to understand things when you see a working example, I have added a simple example that you can use to create hosts, link them to a template and add them to the correct group.

Getting ready

For this recipe, we only need our Zabbix server with the super administrators account that was created at the installation. We need to install the Zabbix agent on the Zabbix server. There is no need to change any of the parameters just make sure that the Zabbix server is monitored by Zabbix. Once it is working, remove the Zabbix server host from the list of hosts in Zabbix as we will add it again by making use of the API.

How to do it...

1. Log into your Zabbix server.

2. Install the EPEL repository as we need `pip` on our machine installed:

   ```
   yum install http://fedora.cu.be/epel/6/i386/epel-release-6-8.
   noarch.rpm
   ```

3. Install `python` and `python-pip` on your Zabbix server as follows:

   ```
   yum install python python-pip
   ```

4. Install the third-party tool **PyZabbix** as follows:

   ```
   pip install pyzabbix
   ```

5. Now create a file called `zabbix_host_add.py` with `vi` or another editor and copy the following code into this file and save it.

6. Alter host parameters where needed:

```python
#!/usr/bin/python
from pyzabbix import ZabbixAPI

# IP of the Zabbix server
ZABBIX_SERVER = 'http://127.0.0.1/zabbix'

# Host Parameters
host_name='Zabbix server'
ip='127.0.0.1'
group='Zabbix servers'
template='Template App Zabbix Server'
port=10050
login='Admin'
password='zabbix'

zapi = ZabbixAPI(ZABBIX_SERVER)

# Login to the Zabbix API
zapi.login(login, password)

group_id = zapi.hostgroup.getobjects(name=group)[0]['groupid']
template_id = zapi.template.getobjects(name=template)[0]
['templateid']

print(group_id)
print(template_id)

zapi.host.create (
    {
        "host": host_name,
        "interfaces":[{
            "type":1,
                "dns":"",
                "main":1,
                "ip": ip,
                "port": port,
                "useip": 1,
        }],
        "groups": [{ "groupid": group_id }],
        "templates": [{ "templateid": template_id }],
    })

print('Host Added')
```

7. Now let's run our script with the following command:

```
python zabbix_host_add.py
```

When the script has run, you should see some output with the `groupid` and the `templateid` parameters and at the last line you will get a message that says: `'Host Added'`.

Now let's go to Zabbix to **Configuration | Hosts** and you should see your Zabbix server back in the list linked with the correct Zabbix template added to the correct group **Zabbix servers**.

How it works...

By making use of PyZabbix, we added a host to our Zabbix server in an easy way. First we defined some parameters such as username, password, hostname, hostgroup, and template. Then we told PyZabbix to authenticate us on the Zabbix server through the API. PyZabbix then gathered the correct ID information for the template and the group we had specified. Next we launched `zapi.host.create` file with all the parameters specified that are necessary to create a new host.

 The API documentation can be really difficult to understand; you probably have to do some trial and error before you understand how it works.

See also

- https://github.com/lukecyca/pyzabbix
- https://www.zabbix.com/documentation/2.4/manual/api/reference

Upgrading and Troubleshooting Zabbix

In this appendix, we will cover:

- Some guidelines to upgrade Zabbix
- Upgrading your Zabbix installation
- Troubleshooting in Zabbix
- Zabbix best practices
- What to expect in Zabbix 3.0
- Zabbix community

Introduction

In this appendix, we will cover a few topics that cannot be placed in a recipe but that are important in order to make optimum use of Zabbix. We will show you some best practices when working with Zabbix and give you some hints on how to troubleshoot when you run into problems. Another important thing to know is how to upgrade your Zabbix installation and what are the problems that you may encounter. We will also see what is coming up in the next version of Zabbix and learn about communities you can seek help from to resolve any issues.

Some guidelines to upgrade Zabbix

First we will talk about some guidelines to follow when you want to upgrade your Zabbix installation.

Zabbix works with a <major>.<minor>.<patch version> numbering. What does this mean? For example, in Zabbix 2.4.1, we have three numbers—the first number is the major version number. So when Zabbix moved from 1.8 to 2.0, we had a major upgrade. The next number is our minor number. The third number is the patch version. Now when we upgrade Zabbix, it is important to know that when the patch version changes, it means that small fixes or small new features are added to Zabbix. Those features never have impact on the database, so updating binaries from your frontend and server alone should be enough.

However, when Zabbix changes the major or the minor number, new features are introduced that have probably made some changes to the database. In this case, it is important to do a database upgrade first.

Also when you download Zabbix you will sometimes see versions that are even and odd. For example, 2.4 and 2.3 releases. The odd releases in Zabbix are the test releases and you should stay away from them in production. The even release is what will be the next release in the future after testing and debugging.

Another important thing to remember is that proxies are like small Zabbix servers. It is important to update your proxies to the same version as your Zabbix server. These components must be upgraded. If you update proxies at later stages, there are chances that you might miss some data which are collecting through the old Zabbix proxy server together.

Agents on the other hand can still work even if they run the most basic version of Zabbix. But don't forget that new versions bring new features, so you probably miss some features and some improvements on stability, memory usage, and so on.

Upgrading your Zabbix installation

You now probably want to know how to upgrade your installation and you probably think it is a painful process, but it isn't! Since version 2.2, upgrading Zabbix is so easy that we will cover the process in no more than a page!

 If you use binaries (you always should in production) then the first thing you need to do is make sure you have a backup in case things go wrong.

There are two ways of upgrading:

1. We can just update the patch version.
2. We can upgrade the major and or minor version in Zabbix.

If you only want to upgrade the minor version (for example, 2.4.0 to 2.4.1) then running an update of your package manager should do the trick, for example, `yum update zabbix*`. Don't forget to restart services once it's done.

If you want to upgrade Zabbix to a new <major> or <minor> verion, for example, 2.2 to 2.4, the follow these steps:

1. Read the release notes just to be sure that noting special needs to be done.
2. Then stop the Zabbix services on your server.
3. Next remove the old binaries.
4. Install the new Zabbix repo as you would for a new installation.
5. Install all Zabbix packages again from the new repo.
6. If you are upgrading from Zabbix 2.0 to 2.2 or from 2.2 to 2.4, everything from here on will be automated. Zabbix will upgrade the database to the new version once you start Zabbix.
7. If you upgrade from Zabbix pre 2.0, then you will have to add database patches first manually, as automated database patching is only available since version 2.2.
8. Next, make sure that your services are on when you restart the server.
9. Zabbix will make a copy of your configuration file, but just to be on the safe side it's probably best to make a copy by yourself before you upgrade. Make sure you change the settings again if you had altered them before you start the server.
10. Make sure proxies are updated at the same time when you upgrade your server. In case if you can't update at the same time, it's advised to stop the server for some time and then update all the proxies, so that this will not break the collection of data.
11. You can now start to upgrade your Zabbix agents.

In the case of SQLite, the database is not upgraded and the common approach is to delete the SQLite database. If you use MySQL or PostgreSQL, the database of the proxy will be upgraded automatically, just as on the Zabbix server.

Troubleshooting in Zabbix

Sometimes Zabbix can be a real pain to troubleshoot if you don't know where to look. Here are some pointers:

- Since Zabbix 2.4 you will now see why your item has failed when you hover your mouse over the red box. This can help you a lot.

- Don't forget that Zabbix logs everything for agent proxy and server under the `/var/log/zabbix/` file. If something fails, this is probably the second place to look at.

- SELinux can mess with your installation too. For example, ping can be blocked by SELinux returning the wrong value as if your host is not reachable. Don't forget that since RHEL 6.5, there are SELinux policies for the agent that can be set as follows:

  ```
  setsebool -P zabbix_can_network on
  ```

- Even if you have set the Boolean, there can be other issues with SELinux. To investigate this you could run:

  ```
  sealert -a /var/log/audit/audit.log
  ```

SELinux will tell you what it has blocked and why, and it will also try to tell you how to undo this. Most of the time this will work however it's not perfect and sometimes you have to investigate further. To make the `sealert` parameter working you probably have to install the `setroubleshoot` package.

For example, creating your own `fping` module could be done like this:

```
grep fping /var/log/audit/audit.log | audit2allow -M zabbix_fping
semodule -i zabbix_fping.pp
```

- Yet another way to solve your problems is by increasing the debug level of the `log` file. However, be careful as increasing the `log` level will give you a lot of information. Since Zabbix 2.4, it is possible to do this without restarting the Zabbix server:

  ```
  zabbix_server -c /etc/zabbix/zabbix_server.conf -R
  log_level_increase
  ```

- This will increase the log level for all services. Same can be done for only the Apache service:

  ```
  zabbix_server -c /etc/zabbix/zabbix_server.conf -R
  log_level_increase="http poller"
  ```

  With the `decrease` option instead of the `increase` option you can return back to log level 3.

- When troubleshooting communication issues between client and server, remember that we have two types of clients. Your client can either be active or passive. In case of an active client, your client needs to be able to connect to port 10051 on the server. In case of a passive client, the server should connect to the client on port 10050. Make sure that both ports can be reached from the client and server. You could use Telnet to test this, for example, `telnet <ip> <port>`.

- If you are running an older version of Zabbix, it could be wise to upgrade. Many bugs are fixed in the latest versions and as we mentioned before, you could gain major speed improvements.

- If you have issues with Zabbix, and you think you have hit a bug, you could have a look at the support page, `https://support.zabbix.com`. Also, feature requests can be made here if you think Zabbix is missing some important feature. If your company is missing an important feature, they can also sponsor this feature by paying Zabbix for the development. (Remember your company saves lots of money by making use of Zabbix that comes for free. This way they could give back to the community and help Zabbix pay for the development.)

- Make sure you make use of **Network Time Protocol** (**NTP**) servers for your Zabbix server and proxies as it can give issues if you run without them. You can identify the issues by looking at your Zabbix queue. It will show you that data is missing for 5, 10 minutes, or more.

- If you encounter a problem when working with SNMP, make sure that your device supports the bulk feature. Some devices don't follow standards well, so the solution in that case could be not to make use of the SNMP bulk feature.

- If monitoring SNMPv3 devices, make sure that `msgAuthoritativeEngineID` (also known as `snmpEngineID` or `"Engine ID"`) is never shared by two devices as this will give rise to problems.

Zabbix best practices

In this section, I would like to share with you some best practices that you can follow when working with Zabbix:

- In general, it's best to work with templates as much as possible.

- Remember that you can make use of macros and define them on template and on host level. So when you create an item in your template, make use of macros as much as possible. This way when you have an item in your template that doesn't work for one of your servers, you don't have to create a second item. Instead, you could just alter the macro on host level.

▶ Zabbix provides a set of standard templates that are too aggressive in my opinion. I suggest that you create your own templates or strip the original ones and only keep what you really need to monitor. Only check items every x number of minutes, instead of seconds, and keep the time interval for history as short as possible. Mostly, there is no need to keep all data for months and for reference most of the time, trends will do just fine.

▶ Often, when I install Zabbix for a customer, I create a new group for the templates that I will use and keep the original Zabbix templates in the template group as reference for later.

▶ Avoid the creation of items directly on hosts. Remember the previous point where I have mentioned making use of macros on template and host.

▶ It's easier to maintain your users when you connect Zabbix to your LDAP or AD.

▶ Remember that permissions are based on the groups and not on user level. Try to make use of groups as much as possible as it's easy to enable / disable them.

What to expect in Zabbix 3.0

▶ First of all, it's important to understand that if you are running Zabbix 2.4, you will lose support from Zabbix as 2.4 is not a long term release such as 2.2. So, it's probably wise to upgrade.

▶ The 2.x series will come to an end, there will be no Zabbix 2.6 coming out, and Zabbix will move on to version 3.0.

▶ So what can we expect from Zabbix version 3.0? So far, it seems that Zabbix 3.0 will continue for focus on improvements. A full overview of what is already added can be found on the Zabbix webpage:

```
http://www.zabbix.org/wiki/Docs/roadmap
```

▶ In 3.0, a major improvement will be full encryption between Zabbix server, clients, and proxies.

▶ SNMP discovery has been improved to support the low-level discovery of multiple OIDs.

▶ Finally, no more dropdown menu for mass editing, enable, disable, and delete. Instead we now have real buttons.

▶ The API has been partially moved to the server side: `http://www.zabbix.org/wiki/Docs/specs/ZBXNEXT-2519#Move_API_to_Zabbix_Server`.

▶ Many other improvements are being made for Zabbix 3.0. A full list of what's new can be found here:

```
https://www.zabbix.com/documentation/3.0/manual/introduction/whatsnew300
```

> ▸ I think that we can expect in the upcoming 3.x releases some interesting improvements, but I will not make any predictions here. To get a good idea what Zabbix will try to improve or add, I suggest you watch Alexei's latest presentation from the Zabbix conference where he points out a few shortcomings and annoyances of Zabbix that he wants to improve over the coming years: `https://www.youtube.com/watch?v=SwuqNIJIb_o`.

Zabbix community

When you have finished the recipes in this book, you should have a good understanding of how Zabbix works, but you will probably also have many more questions on how to monitor certain things in your environment.

I encourage you to join the Zabbix community. Zabbix provides a page where all information is gathered from the community, `http://www.zabbix.com/community.php`.

A lot of information can be found on the Zabbix forums where people have posted questions and received answers for their problems, `http://www.zabbix.com/forum`.

If you would like to help Zabbix improve or write some hacks of your own then you could download the source code, `http://sourceforge.net/projects/zabbix/` or `http://www.zabbix.com/developers.php`.

If you need some quick support, your best bet is probably the IRC `#zabbix` channel on Freenode, where lots of people check in every day, including most of the Zabbix developers: `http://webchat.freenode.net/?channels=#zabbix`.

Most importantly, don't forget to check out the website `www.zabbix.org` where people from the community contribute all their knowledge. If you have made some templates or if you have created some interesting hacks such as *Action simulator* project, that tells you why you were not notified by Zabbix, then this is the page for you to share your knowledge with the rest of the community. After all, that's what open source is all about!

If you live in Belgium, then you could join our Zabbix Meetup group where people talk about their Zabbix setup or other interesting things they have done with Zabbix. Feel free to join to learn more or to host a meeting to show us your Zabbix project: `http://www.meetup.com/Belgian-Zabbix-User-Group/`.

Index

Z

Zabbix
about 195, 225
administration 62
advanced triggers 139
architecture 41-44
best practices 229, 230
configuring, for VMware 178, 179
definitions 37-39
definitions, URL 40
devices, creating in 198-201
hosts 37
hosts, adding 37-39
installing, from source 17-20
log files, testing 134-137
monitoring 213, 214
reference links 218
trigger constructor, using 137
troubleshooting 228, 229
URL, for agent communication 76
URL, for documentation 16
URL, for macros 130
URL, for manual 18, 21
URL, for simple checks 82
URL, for support 98
URL, for UserParameter 80

Zabbix 2.4
URL 32

Zabbix 3.0
defining 230, 231

Zabbix agent
configuring 7-9
extending 78, 79
installing 7-9

Zabbix agent configuration file,
Unix / Windows
references 9

Zabbix API 219, 220

Zabbix community
about 231
references 231

Zabbix documentation
URL 28, 69, 214

Zabbix frontend
about 27
exploring 27-36
working 37

Zabbix installation
upgrading 226, 227

zabbix_sender tool
about 92-94
reference link 95

Zabbix server
configuring 1-6
installing 1-6
installing, in distributed setup 21-26
options, passing to UserParameter 79, 80
URL 192

Zabbix Server SLA 176

Zabbix upgrade
guidelines 226

Zabbix web interface
configuring 10-16
frontend installation 10-16

Thank you for buying
Zabbix Cookbook

About Packt Publishing

Packt, pronounced 'packed', published its first book, *Mastering phpMyAdmin for Effective MySQL Management*, in April 2004, and subsequently continued to specialize in publishing highly focused books on specific technologies and solutions.

Our books and publications share the experiences of your fellow IT professionals in adapting and customizing today's systems, applications, and frameworks. Our solution-based books give you the knowledge and power to customize the software and technologies you're using to get the job done. Packt books are more specific and less general than the IT books you have seen in the past. Our unique business model allows us to bring you more focused information, giving you more of what you need to know, and less of what you don't.

Packt is a modern yet unique publishing company that focuses on producing quality, cutting-edge books for communities of developers, administrators, and newbies alike. For more information, please visit our website at www.packtpub.com.

About Packt Open Source

In 2010, Packt launched two new brands, Packt Open Source and Packt Enterprise, in order to continue its focus on specialization. This book is part of the Packt open source brand, home to books published on software built around open source licenses, and offering information to anybody from advanced developers to budding web designers. The Open Source brand also runs Packt's open source Royalty Scheme, by which Packt gives a royalty to each open source project about whose software a book is sold.

Writing for Packt

We welcome all inquiries from people who are interested in authoring. Book proposals should be sent to author@packtpub.com. If your book idea is still at an early stage and you would like to discuss it first before writing a formal book proposal, then please contact us; one of our commissioning editors will get in touch with you.

We're not just looking for published authors; if you have strong technical skills but no writing experience, our experienced editors can help you develop a writing career, or simply get some additional reward for your expertise.

Mastering Zabbix

ISBN: 978-1-78328-349-1   Paperback: 358 pages

Monitor your large IT environment efficiently with Zabbix

1. Create the perfect monitoring configuration based on your specific needs.

2. Extract reports and visualizations from your data.

3. Integrate monitoring data with other systems in your environment.

4. Learn the advanced techniques of Zabbix to monitor networks and performances in large environments.

Zabbix 1.8 Network Monitoring

ISBN: 978-1-84719-768-9   Paperback: 428 pages

Monitor your network's hardware, servers, and web performance effectively and efficiently

1. Start with the very basics of Zabbix, an enterprise-class open source network monitoring solution, and move up to more advanced tasks later.

2. Efficiently manage your hosts, users, and permissions.

3. Get alerts and react to changes in monitored parameters by sending out e-mails, SMSs, or even execute commands on remote machines.

4. In-depth coverage for both beginners and advanced users with plenty of practical, working examples and clear explanations.

Please check **www.PacktPub.com** for information on our titles

CPSIA information can be obtained
at www.ICGtesting.com
Printed in the USA
LVOW03s1929101115

461901LV00007B/245/P